Remnants of the Disappeared:

A Memoir

by Amy Waugh

To Brad:
My goofy, erratic, divine mystery that words could never contain but my heart will, always. These pages are my past - now we all rage on to an unknowable future...
P.S. - I owe you $50! :)
XO,
Amy

Cover design by Wendy Metcalf
Photo credit: Ian Kimmer

©2014 Red Orchid Press   Des Moines, IA

"I tell you this
to break your heart,
by which I mean only
that it break open and never close again
to the rest of the world."
- Mary Oliver

PROLOGUE: RECESS

You remember them, don't you?

The ones who "got away." The memories that flicker at their edges and cast shadows so large that you cannot be sure whether or not they are real at all?

Strip yourself naked. Sit down on the edge of the tub in the bathroom's garish fluorescent light. Examine every millimeter of flesh for scars and see if you can't recall the memories of them.

Point proudly at your kneecap and exclaim to no one: That one!

I was six, you say to the empty room. It was recess. I was running.

You find yourself grinning a six-year-old's grin, the exhaust fan the wind in your hair.

And then your forehead starts to furrow. Who, or what? Were you running to or from?

You take a deep breath, run your hand down your smooth shin. You exhale.

The pavement, you think. It was blacktop. Brand new. Your resolve strengthens with the details.

And the blood. It was so bright. But I didn't tell anybody. I was limping, but I couldn't tell. There was something I needed to do first.

Wait. Did I go find Mrs. S? Or did she find me? Force upon me a rinse and a band-aid, a phone call to Mom...

Was that the day we made butterflies out of tinfoil to hang on the tree? Or the stained glass window ornament to bring home to our parents?

One of the bulbs over the vanity mirror flickers. It jars you. You remember that you are naked. An adult. Alone in a white bathroom. Your present moment is completely exposed: every minute detail. But your past eludes you like the last drag of a cigarette.

That sharp, civil twinge – and then gone.

"Nothing is built on stone; all is built on sand, but we must build as if the sand were stone."

- Jorge Luis Borges

PART I: FRACTURES

When the marrow of the mind is breached by trauma, its instinct is to fracture, like bone. What was life's narrative becomes multiple narratives – compartmentalized, divided by deep fissures that it becomes hard to leap across. It's a kind of punctual equilibrium, marked by traumatic events: divorce, sexual assault, murder…the loss of an infant; the self-inflicted death of a friend.

One tries to remember the times before and the times in between, but recall remains shaky. I try to tell the story of even the day before my world was fractured, but instead land somewhere in Colorado, at the breakfast table when I was five, my mother mashing up fried eggs for me, a chocolate milk mustache on my upper lip. Instinctually, I retreat to where it is safe – or at least, every day, I try. And safe is always backwards, toward some mirage-like image of home. Toward the outstretched arms of a mother who is still waiting for me to come to my senses.

Moving forward in the world would be so much easier if I were salmon, and so I read about them, study them, but can't quite get it right. However, I insist it is possible to find it: the exact place where I started this journey. And so I am forever trying to get back there, but GPS is no help when it's one's own mind one is trying to navigate.

Where did I store the time when a young man asked my permission to be kissed? What did I wear? What was the temperature outside? Where were we standing – sidewalk or grass? Where is that girl, who was willing to believe in any fairytale that came along? Maybe it's good that she's gone.

Somewhere in a box in Mom's attic or underneath my bed there's a picture of me in a green velvet dress. It's a Renaissance pattern with long sleeves, a braided maroon and silver belt with tassels. Senior prom. I wanted to be Lady Guinevere, or a lady in waiting. If you discounted the steel-toed Doc Marten combat boots underneath. Next to me is a young man with ruddy cheeks and curly brown hair. His face is boyish, mischievous. He wears an impish grin that radiates there above the black suit, a dimple in his left cheek. My arm is threaded through Brian's arm. My smile coy and uncertain.

I can pinpoint the moment the fracture occurred – but unlike the time when my car hit a guardrail, metal smashing against metal, bone against glass – there was no audible shattering. I had just been raped one month prior, and lain in bed for nearly a month with mono: immune system and support system – all of it crashing. And then my rock, my best friend, my man with the barrel chest and strong arms and sweet boyish face – the love of my young life so far – then I found out he was involved in a murder. No greenstick fracture, this one, unbelievably compound.

I understood, now, why his shoulders were so bent and mine bent too, buckled under all this weight. They had taken him away – the whole story a long one, a wrong place/wrong time, but still very wrong one. They had taken him away and I tried to be myself, the girl with impermeable armor, the self I had been since seven and my mother needed me to. I talked down the girlfriends of the other men involved, I talked in circles, chain smoked 'til dawn. I hadn't slept for what seemed like days. Ten years now, and I still remember the moment something broke inside my head and I let grief take me. Grief for everything just lost – my only safe place since the sexual assault, and maybe in my whole young life – was in his arms, and now they were gone, too. I shut the door to some common room, and slid down it in tears. Someone must have carried me, hauled me, helped me eventually, to bed, but all I remember is blackness. I felt the break in my brain and I let the pain take me.

Somewhere in a red box in the attic or the storage closet or the corner of my underwear drawer there's a dried white corsage that I haven't touched in years. Perhaps the petals have all fallen off now, sweetening and scenting the contents of the box. Certainly they have browned and become brittle.

And the straight pin stuck through the stem of it has started to rust; the pearl on the end of it has chipped to reveal the dull gray plastic under-neath.

When he told me the story of the events that would lead to his arrest, Brian and I sat on a wooden dock on a small pond on the campus of Northwest Missouri State University. My legs, laden down with the weight of the same toes I wore to prom, hung heavy toward the murky water. The October night was cool and I wanted a sweater. I wanted to listen to that song Brian always played for me when he deejayed at the college radio station. *Everything's going to be alright, rock-a-bye.* But I could only rock myself back and forth on the dock, trying to tune out the confirmation of the rumor, to veer my life away from another moment in which everything would change, but it was too late. The moment had already passed.

Ten years. To the day? I don't know. But my body remembers and recoils every year around this time. Fall. My favorite weather. My birthday. What should be enjoyable and full of beauty instead makes me lethargic, lonely, suddenly full of fear. The nights get long. I used to love more than anything, even as a child, walking the streets at night – the quiet suburban sidewalks. The stars, the night sky – my father and I would gaze at them together. We would drink root beer in glass bottles and choose our future homes in heaven, looking for the light that would signify the remaining love of those already gone.

"That one is Jennifer's," he would say to me, his finger in an arc toward the sky. "And that one is your grandfathers – he's been looking down on you since before you were born. And that one, someday, will be mine where I'll wait for you."

It might have been a slightly morbid ritual, but I still love the stars, and sleeping under them – except that now my nighttime walks are interrupted by sudden bouts of fear in which I sprint home as fast as I can from some unknown pursuer. This affliction – it hasn't gone away, and perhaps it never will. In truth, there's no sense to it. I was sexually assaulted in the middle of the afternoon, not at some nighttime drunken party. But somehow I think it has to do with safety, with the nonexistence of such a thing. Times were I thought I had healed, but grief is a repeating cycle. I know that demons can't be ignored, but haven't yet figured how to slay them. I'm trying, instead, to incorporate them. It may be the labyrinth to beat all mazes. As Tori Amos says, "I can't seem to find my way out of this hunting ground..." And it *is* a feeling of being hunted. Being blamed, feeling guilty. Wishing for a flaming arrow to just pierce my heart once and for all and let it set itself on fire. Wishing to rise from ashes, like a phoenix – but first, how to become ash?

Somewhere in a box is a photo of two faces: Brian and I, close up, cheek to cheek. My sunglasses are resting on top of my dark hair, and I am looking up at him. Loki is grinning for the lens, for the imprint on the film he knows he will make: those two charming dimples, those incorrigible curls. Just before that night on the dock I had thought I had arrived at the beginning of something. It was Halloween and it was our first night together. But it was also one of the last. Two weeks later the cops pulled him from class and his mouth was already halfway open before he was through the doorway, those words choked back on the dock now ready to spill over again and again until he could absolve himself of them. For seven years, we didn't speak, but I'm trying now to fill in the blanks. I'm trying to do what I can with the words I have been given because this is not my story.

From prison, Brian still writes me letters – still claims to feel something called love. But who is he after all these years? I am not the girl he loved, and never will be again. Vengeance saw to that, and sorrow, heavy as wet cement. There was a brief time of promises, but not a single one remains that I can keep. We got to be young and in love once. There was that. Loki. Pander. The Trickster. How do I tell him we are both prisoners now? Me, of my late night mind, my nightmares, my flashbacks in the arms of other lovers who haven't done a thing to hurt me and yet I hurt all over again and again and again. My newly concussed brain that never found a bridge over the trauma and now has physical trauma to compound its situation. A body that constantly betrays. Memories that can't cohere. Even if I could give you everything, I would say, all I have left are pieces. And I've labored at the card table over this puzzle for hours, but the pieces will never fit.

In the beginning there was a child. The White Coats took the child and put her in an incubator. There was light. The child did not like the light. She missed the water and the darkness of the water. She missed the way her whole world was defined solely through the sense of touch, although she did not know how to ar-ticulate this yet. The child screamed, but the White Coats could not hear her through the Plexiglas. Only her mother heard the screaming, or rather felt it: a dull throbbing in her abdomen. Her womb, like the sea, still felt echoes of the life it so recently held. It undulated with a force as strong as rage. She sang to the child, but the sound did not penetrate the incubator where the infant lay. The mother's voice was lost in the bright white air.

Somewhere in Colorado

In Colorado, in the community I was to be raised in, the towns were named for the land. Basalt, after the rock. Aspen, after the trees. Marble, Crystal City, Glenwood Springs. Our back yard was connected to the mountain behind it. When I looked out of our living room window, the chain link fence dissolved in my line of vision and all the land was one. In winter, when snow covered the fences, my eyes could travel up the line of white as it rose steadily up Basalt Mountain until it finally stopped at blue. That blue was a place I knew I'd get to someday. It was a blue that shimmered as if it were the mountain's aura; the sun reflecting off the land above snow line gave the horizon around it an extra glow. It was a blue reminiscent of sapphire, my birthstone, shining on my mother's ring finger, the last of three.

Basalt is a volcanic rock that makes up most of the sea floor. The rock formation that rose out of my yard was once part of the sea. An acre of land served as my backyard, and the mountains were attached to it. The backyard is the place where children dream and play. I never saw the mountains as being separate from it.

For what were the mountains there for if not to explore, to climb? In the yard where I sat on a swing and kicked my pink sneakers toward the sapphire blue horizon, a billion protozoa once swam through swift currents toward a far more distant horizon. An ancient community teemed with life, whose ultimate goal was diversity. They swam towards a complex world that would con-tain the things that adhere to a child's memory: the fragrance of lilacs, sunlight glinting off of snow, playground chains pressing into her palms.

Our home in the Rocky Mountains, our perfect square acre of land, consisted of a fruit orchard, a vegetable garden, a row of Aspen trees and Columbine bushes out front. Large lilac bushes grew next to the patio, filling the air with their scent. Hummingbird feeders hung in at least three of our windows. Apple Drive. Basalt, Colorado. We were a small community nestled at the banks of the Roaring Fork River, ten miles from Aspen. Our road was long and made from gravel. A mile down, across from the bus stop, someone had horses, and my sister and I would climb the split-rail fence to feed them apples. Coyotes often howled at our back fence. I heard them in my dreams.

A drainage ditch from the neighboring farm ran through our backyard. At its banks, I collected earthworms with a boy whose name I've forgotten. He ate one once to try to impress me with four-year-old bravado. And he must have, in his way. Another boy, or maybe the same one, the son of my parents' friends, showed me his penis while we were playing with matchbox cars. I don't remember if I told, but I do remember thinking that it looked like an earthworm – pale and vulnerable and trying to escape.

Back then, the children of my parents' friends were always around. We built castles in the giant tire that served as a sandbox, jumped on twin beds to Michael Jackson songs, and rode a denim beanbag down the stairs to the basement where our parents would scowl at us from over the tops of their gin and tonics or seven and sevens. I didn't have any concept of it then, but our parents were the upper middle class of Aspen society: architects and bankers trying to make it big. They held parties at which they hoped those from the Hollywood film industry would attend, and for weeks after, they would gush about meeting Goldie Hawn's hair stylist or the guy who wrote the score to "The Champ."

And some of our parents were almost famous themselves. When the parents held parties, the kids would have sleepovers, and Laura Podolak's were always the best. Laura and I waited for the school bus together. Her dad was a retired quarterback for the Kansas City Chiefs. When she hosted sleepovers, we had scavenger hunts in the labyrinth of their house and watched movies on the biggest TV I had ever seen. Little girls lined up in My Little Pony sleeping bags, an endless supply of popcorn and M&Ms. But of course, Laura had a real pony, too. Our families, then, were adhered to each other by their shared dreams. Some of the dreams came true, but most of them faded away.

We had come to Colorado when I was six months old, a family of four loaded up into a tan buick, a golden retriever called Rocky. You see, my father, Wayne, was in love with the West. He was born in Iowa, the same state as his hero, John Wayne. The youngest of three boys, he was practical by nature but always possessed a dreamy spark of idealism shining in the corner of his eye. He married young, a handsome man in an Air Force uniform, and fathered five children. The youngest of these, his only son: John Wayne Clark. My uncle's name is John, so under duress, he'd claim to have named his son after family. The practical thing to do. But in reality, poor young Johnny was named for a dream that his mother wouldn't follow, that would fail his father in the end.

 This was before I came into the picture. My father left his first wife and met my mother while she was working at his bank. Thirteen years younger than he was, pretty and petite, he saw a glint of mischief in her eyes as she passed around a tray of chocolate-covered ants and bees, a practical joke from the women to the men. This bit of mischief he knew, he recognized. So they married: he in a baby blue leisure suit, she in a purple flowered dress, her beehive rising halfway to the ceiling. He adopted her two-year old daughter.

 Between them, they now had six children, but she wanted another. For five years she wore him down, while they both lost their fathers to cancer and heart disease. And then Jennifer was born, not breathing. My father took it as a sign to quit, but my mother was lost in grief. And so six years after their marriage and many arguments later, I finally came along into the mugginess of a Midwestern fall, a full six weeks ahead of schedule. And as I started to crawl across the green shag carpet (which I swear is my first memory), it was decided that I would not grow up in this place. That my father would follow the old creed, "Go west, young man," his new family in tow. It was decided that all of their unrealized dreams would be pinned on me.

So they packed the tan Buick. Baby on mama's lap. Little girl with her palms pressed to the glass in the back. Rocky, the Golden Retriever, pacing the seat beside her. Father at the helm, steering the ship towards the New World, where all of the answers were waiting…

I am told that when I was two years old I toddled into the living room of our Colorado home and climbed into my Grandmother's lap. My mass of dark brown hair was wild and tangled from a nap. Playing with her blouse buttons, I innocently asked her age.

"Sixty-one," she replied.

I looked at her in all earnestness and said, "When people get old, they die."

My grandmother lived with us, then. In an apartment attached to our big, brick house. I was too young to remember, really, but I imagine her holding my hand, walking me to the bus for preschool. Handing me a plastic trowel to help her dig in the garden. Pulling up squash and leaf lettuce. Snapping green beans into a colander at the picnic table. Baking zucchini bread, mon-key bread, banana nut bread.

These scenes, I imagine them in time-lapse photography. My long hair in a braid as I sit next to my grandmother on the worn red picnic table, watching my own children play on the land they have inherited, the sun setting behind the mountain in a haze of purples and pinks. But it wasn't to be. When people get old, they die. My grandmother is eighty-five now, and she loves to retell this story. To remind me that I am her "weird" grandchild: the only one to go to college, the only one to move away. Yet she also likes to remind me how I have inherited her hands. And when I sit with her, she strokes my long, slender fingers with her own.

My grandmother was one of three tenants who lived in the apartment attached to our house. She was the first, my aunt and young cousin were the second, and my half-brother Johnny was the third. All in transition, for one reason or another, the members of my family flocked to our home for shelter and stability. My grandmother after selling her house, my aunt after leaving her abusive boyfriend, my brother a young man trying to find himself. And although I was still a child, I understood why they envied us, why ours was a life to look up to. At least, from the outside. And children are outsiders, always – placed there for protection, though it often wounds them more. For children have the burden of having no burdens at all. Every injury is fresh, with no prior experience to compare it to. And thus those first hurts stick with us in ways that will never repeat themselves again.

For how could I know, then, that Mom wouldn't always be out in the dirt on her knees tending the vegetable garden? That there wouldn't always be windfall apples to feed the horses in September, and a brand new swing set gleaming in the sun. No one told me to memorize the howls of the coyotes or the angles of the mountains as they met the sky. Or to have a good time at Laura's next sleepover, because it might be the last I'd have in that big, beautiful house. And my parents didn't fight in front of us, as far as I can remember. I imagine they were just lost in their own dreams, too, until they realized that they weren't dreaming the same ones anymore. None of us ever really imagines life without each other until it happens, and all we have are photographs and a child's memories of sweets and songs and sun.

The child was lonely in the Plexiglas box, but she was un-harmed. She had no scars like the one on her mother's belly to mark the moment when she entered the light. Her skin was soft and white and pure. She was not used to the way the world felt without the pressure of the dark water surrounding it. She was not used to the shadows that fell over her hairless head every time a White Coat leaned over her.

Any Fairytale That Came Along

When I was very young, I exerted a tremendous amount of will power over my tiny body. At two, I scraped my knee while running down the driveway. Bits of skin and blood were embedded in the concrete. My mother called out to me. Arms outstretched, she ran toward her toddler to scoop me in her arms and quiet the tears that weren't falling.

Instead, I yelled, "I'm fine!" as my precious, precocious knees pumped my two-foot frame farther and farther away from her.

We laugh about that story now, and retell it at family gatherings, but secretly it haunts me. In it, I see echoes of a girl whose stubbornness would nearly kill her, and who would lose so many more bits of skin and blood along the way.

At seven, in second grade, I sat at my desk, forehead beaded with a cold sweat, my stomach flipping its contents over and over as I completed a worksheet on subtraction. Eventually, I stood on shaky legs and wandered up to the line in front of the teacher's desk, for those who had questions. When my turn came, I managed to get out only my teacher's name, before my hand flew up to my mouth, thick orange vomit the color of her hair flooding out through the spaces between my fingers.

This instinct to hold back, to be "self-contained," where did it come from? My mother insists that as an infant I was the right mix of needy and content. That I once loved being held, and cherished affection the way most children do. But in my own memories, I only remember pushing her, and everyone else, away.

My first crush was a boy named Josh. We were the same age, but he was one grade below me. I was in tenth, he was in ninth. He wore a vintage brown leather jacket even in the dead of summer. He had gone to Christian school and then been homeschooled, and so had only just arrived at our public high school of about four thousand students. He brooded, smoked cigarettes, snuck off to the gas station during lunchtime to roll a joint. He belonged to a different era. I wanted to belong to a different anything.

    I wrote poems for him and stuck them in his jacket pockets. He received them, but we didn't speak, much. I was convinced that my love was radiating at such a rate that he would absorb it merely by inhabiting the same room, the same row of desks in Drama class. But his eyes remained downcast. He wandered the halls aloof, seeming to exist in a world in which he felt loved by no one. The only acknowledgement of my declarations came in the form of a simple "Thanks." And a crooked smile.

    Eventually, though, we became friends. We smoked pot at our friend's house, the one whose parents were too cool to be parents and enabled opportunities such as these. He'd stand in the driveway mesmerized by the headlights on her car. Like a conductor, he'd lift and lower his arms as the lights rose and then retreated into their metal casing, over and over, like Morse code transmitting into the dark.

As our friendship developed, I learned he collected Star Wars figurines. Once, in passing, he mentioned how he'd been looking for years for the Luke Skywalker with the gold medallion he's presented with at the end of Return of the Jedi. I searched the area shops until I found it, this perfect gift. And as he drove me home, high, from our friend's house in the middle of a blizzard one night, I presented him with it, for his birthday. He looked out the window, on the verge of tears. He set the small paper sack gently on the dashboard. The porch light was on. My parents were waiting. I fidgeted in the seat, shifting my weight back and forth between my hipbones. He was supposed to kiss me now. It was all supposed to fall into place. Instead, he continued to look away, Adam's apple bobbing slightly in his throat. I thought of how his face would look from the other side of the glass: frozen like Luke's behind the plastic casing. And perhaps he did feel trapped – needed me to reach out and take his hand. Instead, I retreated into my own packaging, and got out of the car with a falsely bright farewell.

The next crush was a jazz saxophone player. He stood before the bleachers in his black leather trench coat, blowing out every note of "My Funny Valentine" in my direction. It took two years of him sneaking into the library during my history class's research sessions, pestering me, stalking me through the aisles of books, for me to finally agree to go on a date with him. But eventually I relented, I began to unfurl. He was my first kiss, my first notion of something resembling love.

So I wrote poems for him, too. In mottled black composition notebooks, with purple ink. I'd sneak them into his palm as he came through my checkout line at the local drugstore. His five-foot-five frame, his flat feet shuffling over the tiled floor. His voice, affected to sound like Christian Slater's, ordering a pack of Kamel Reds. Everything he did was languorous, leisurely. His fingers were squared and stubby. His body was like that of a prepubecent boy, even at seventeen.

And then he went to college. Another one lost, to games where he role-played vampires. To friends who would end up in prison. To a dead-end job fixing instruments in Kansas, getting gigs wherever he could find them. I hear he's married now, and maybe he still plays. For his wife, for his friends. But when I imagine the scene, his playing lacks the intensity, the passion he displayed when he played for me.

I choose to forget the name of the third crush. His dorm room walls of avocado green. His long blond ponytail. His father, who threw him down the stairs, beat his back with a belt. His plaid sheets, stained with my blood.

I choose to forget the way he looked at me with such sudden disdain, such disappointment that the love he'd always needed wasn't there. A worthless piece of shit, he called me. That much I remember. And the rough way he handled my small frame.

Perhaps because of that love he needed; because I wasn't big enough to hold it.

A few weeks later, after walking out of his dorm room for the last time, I found out I had contracted mononucleosis. A common virus that affects nearly everyone, it has become an adolescent rite of passage.

"It's possible," the doctor said, "that your spleen could rupture. You need to rest for at least six weeks."

Instead of being frightened, I clutched at that knowledge. Something in me had been welling up, and I held onto that word, *rupture*. I had hours available in which to write, but I'd put the pen away. The notebooks were shoved to the back of my desk drawer. Words weren't helping anymore. With waning energy I pushed my short legs up and down the four flights of stairs, hoping for a miracle. The same legs that once carried a toddler away from the mother who was trying to protect her were still exercising their right to free will. Excused from classes, I walked the long eleven blocks to the movie theater every day - sure that at any moment, that elusive organ, the spleen, would split at the seams, fluids rushing out to fill up my empty spaces.

A few months later, my first real boyfriend carried me in his arms out of my childhood bedroom and into my parents' living room. I had woken up in agony, my right knee shot through with pain. I did not cry out, but my breath came in ragged gasps, the pain rolling in waves that eroded away at my sinews with such speed and precision it left chasms in its wake. Between breaths, I pleaded with the pain to envelop me, to pull me into a void so complete it would absorb all emptiness and I'd come out complete and unscathed. But the pain passed with the night. No cause was ever found.

And I realized then that it was my own fault, that each breath was a choice. That if I tried, I could accomplish much more than brief bursts of fury. I knew then, what Anne Sexton had meant in her poem, "Wanting to Die." That suicides have a special language. That: *To thrust all that life under your tongue!/ that, all by itself, becomes a passion.*

In high school, I spent summer nights locked in the bathroom with a book, a tub full of lukewarm water, and the blade from my dissection kit for biology class. My mother and stepfather would be out for the night drinking margaritas or playing nickel slots and I would be, as I had always preferred it, alone. Tentative at first, I'd gently drag the sharp edge over my skin, the same line over and over until a few drops of blood found their way to the surface.

That was my first habit. My mother and sister shredded their fingernails; I shredded my skin. And over the years I found myself moving on from razor blades, from small superficial wounds. Nights -- I'd curl into a ball, insides twisted and wrought with worry. In moments of lucidity between drug-induced states, I'd formulate my escape. And I'll never really be sure how the decision was made, but I eventually found myself sitting in the back room of some café downing sixteen blue sleeping pills with a large mug of coffee. Stumbling into the pastel painted bricks of the doorframe on my way out to the street. A dead crow on the sidewalk, one glazed black eye meeting mine. The hushed phone call from another room. The bright lights of the ER, frowning faces swimming in and out of focus.

In the morning, two fingers rested gently on the thin skin of my wrist. My pulse was present, thready and weak. My eyes slid open, peered through the fog into the face of my poetry professor's husband. And it came flooding back: the shift I'd missed at work as a waitress where the same professor's band was scheduled to play. Their worried eyes darting around the large, dusty bar – because until that day I had been punctual, and never missed a shift.

I retreated into darkness, pretended not to recognize him. And when I saw him around, later, he never brought it up. He was skilled at hiding the questions in his eyes. But his voice was softer, his tone more imploring. "How are you?" he'd say, and my cheeks would flame with shame. I had been telling myself it didn't happen. But the slight tilt of his head told me it did. All that life under my tongue. Or rather, on top of it. And my own slender fingers had placed it there.

Mea culpa, mea culpa, mea maxima culpa. Father forgive me, Mother...

"This guilt you carry, this grief - it's like a broken leg," my psychiatrist explained. "One that's healed crookedly. We'll have to go back and re-break it in order to put it together correctly."

But I couldn't afford his treatments. Or so I told myself. I rocked back and forth in the big leather chair, staring out the window at the highway. His forefinger in a perfect curl above his upper lip. This was his thinking pose. He was willing to wait it out, to wait for me to tell my story. He was the first since the fracture to offer up flat open palms on which I could place my burdens. But I was paying him for this, I reminded myself. And that broken leg, crooked or not, it had healed. Wasn't that what he had said?

By the time the child left the box she was accustomed to space and silence. She did not cry to be held or touched. The child lay in her crib, her eyes scanning the patterns of the soft yellow light on the pale blue walls, saving the image in her head of the play of lights and shadows. This image would stay with her. It would always remind her of water; of the soft, wet darkness of her original home.

But this is not my story...

Her name was Gracie Hixon. She was sixty-six years old. She had a daughter, if I remember right, a husband called Clyde. Sixty-six and still working. Late nights at the Stop-N-Go. They must have been just scraping by. Perhaps her husband received disability, social security. Perhaps she had been a housewife and accrued no retirement fund of her own.

That day, from what I gather, the three boys were experimenting with cocaine. Tony, Brian, Peter. For two of them, anyway, it was a new experience, some excitement in that small Missouri town. They were going to do a grab and go. Kid stuff. Empty backpacks full of Doritos and snacks and laughing all the way home. Tony needed something out of the trunk, pulled out a shotgun Brian could see in the rearview mirror. Brian, Loki, frozen in the front seat while the other two went inside, went inside and came back out with the snacks and enough money for a night's drinking anyway. Brian breathing again because it was OK, no one was hurt and then Tony halting in mid-motion as he opened the passenger door saying: *Wait, she saw my face. She saw my face.*

What do gunshots sound like? What does an old woman's face look like after it's hit with a 12-gauge sawed off shotgun from ten inches away? How loud was the silence after the shot? How loud is it still?

When the child was a toddler, there was a crystal that hung in her bedroom window. It was quartz, which is prismatic, and it cast a play-of-colors on her light blue walls. The child began to recognize that there was more to the water than extreme darkness and bright light. She began to imagine herself under the surface of the bath, rainbows dancing on the small swells of the water. She wanted to move the bath into her bedroom. She wanted to touch the rainbows, but they were just out of her reach.

The Mirage-like Image of Home

When I am in second grade, the mountains fade from the rear view as Mom packs the Plymouth Voyager and takes her girls down from the mountain. We come to inhabit a state that looks like graph paper from an airplane. Each agricultural plot is nearly identical. The only thing that juts into the horizon is the Woodmen Building in the Omaha skyline, across the Missouri River. We have crickets in the basement, water beetles in the bathroom. Every time it rains, it floods, ruining items from my past one by one. Grandmother's rocking chair, the couch I had lain sick on, board games, Christmas decorations, a framed family photo. I learn about sump pumps, learn to pile beloved items on the curb and call them "trash." A tornado hit in 1988, three months after we moved. The neighbor's sycamore tree toppled over and was inches from our front door. The Venetian blinds flapped in the wind as my sister and I ran downstairs, even though the windows were barely cracked. A house three blocks away was ripped from its foundation as the family of four huddled in the basement beneath it – confirming my instincts that nothing here was solid, like the mountains we had left. That in this wide open landscape, there would be no place to take shelter from the forces that could tear a family apart.

In the deep southwestern corner of Colorado is a place called Mesa Verde. In Spanish, it means "the green table." Back in the Buick, we traveled there on a summer trip. We rode a black locomotive from Silverton to Durango – a refurbished steam train that ran along a very old rail line that forged one of the first pathways into the mythical "West." The windows were open to the air and my cousin got a cinder in his eye. In Durango, we stopped at a souvenir shop and I filled my pockets with iron pyrite, hematite, tiger's eye, purple quartz – mineral samples polished to a sheen that I wasn't aware was unnatural. A lacquer brushed onto synthetic stones. But something about them had always attracted me. I'd line my child-sized white bookshelves with them and beg for a small bag full at every small shop we entered.

 The metallic sheen of hematite was my favorite. Hematite is iron oxide, a liquid form of rust that has been pressurized for millions of years. Because it has no cleavage planes, the stones they sell in mineral shops are generally spherical or ovoid. Mine was smooth and egg-shaped. I liked to flip it around in my palm. I felt safe with it in my pocket.

 Hematite is said to purify the blood when placed over certain areas of the body. Perhaps this is because it contains iron and turns dark red when crushed. Thus the name: hema(o) meaning blood in Latin. And perhaps this is why I have always been attracted to it: a shimmering sphere that looks as if it could have come from outer space, but when crushed turns into a pile of blood red rust.

Every summer, our family would take a trip: to Mt. Rushmore, the Grand Canyon, Disneyland, or fishing in Canada's boundary waters. Too young to recall most of these outings, I have to rely on fragments and photographs: my sister holding me up as I sit on a stone wall in South Dakota, a line of newly hatched ducks following their mother down to the water, my tiny three year old body perched on Dad's shoulders in front of the Enchanted Castle.

 What I do remember is Dad waking us at three in the morning, the suitcases sitting by the door from the night before, the dim light of the front hallway. We'd enter into the garage and climb into the car, pillows stuffed under arms, blankets trailing behind. A few hours later, as the sun woke us, I'd hear Dad humming "Moon River" in the front seat. Next to him, Mother's head lolled sideways on her foam neck rest, softly snoring. I was curled in the corner, while my sister hogged most of the back seat.

 Seeing me, bored and lonely in the rearview mirror, Dad would stop humming and start singing me songs. "Amy says find a little lake, find a little lake, find a little lake." And I'd look out the window, trying my best. "There's one, daddy!" But it was just standing water. No fish resided there, only mosquitoes, breeding in the stagnant green-brown water, preparing to swarm.

The origins of the word "stagnate" come from the Latin "stagnatum" which means "standing water." Like the lakes I thought I saw through the car window as the highway rolled on underneath us. Phil Collins, in his old band Genesis, wrote a song about stagnation: *And I will wait forever, beside the silent mirror, and fish for better minnows amongst the weeds and slimy water.* And I want to think that this is part of the reason my mother left my father: to fish for better minnows. Or perhaps she was just plain tired of fishing.

But I wasn't ready yet. My young life had not yet reached a point of stagnation. I wanted to understand her reasons, but couldn't escape my own perceptions. I had bigger fish to catch. I had hours left to spend at my father's side, legs swinging over the edge of the boat. And she took me away, to the cornfields of her youth. To a place where the only water was the rushing, muddy Missouri River. Its stench and strong undertow. And the stagnant pools that formed in the fields after each hard rain. The breeding grounds for mosquitoes, who waited for me to come out at night, so they could suck out any hope that was left in my tender flesh.

Mesa Verde was not at all green, as far as I can remember. Spruce trees and shrubs surround the park, but they do not grow in my memory. The landscape that arises there inhabits various shades of red and brown, dust and stone, a palette of desert colors. There were wooden ladders leading down into holes in the earth where sacred ceremonies were once performed. Elaborate buildings built into the sides of cliffs, each clay brick placed there by weatherworn hands. I remember wandering around behind my mother, a beaded headband around my forehead. My skin was dark from summer play at high altitudes, and I imagined myself a young Anasazi child. I wanted to climb down the ladder into the darkness. To grab a hammer stone and pulverize the hematite in my pocket until I could sift the blood red remnants through my fingers before mixing them into clay. I imagined I would sit cross-legged on the floor of the kiva, while my mother worked the clay into a pot, long braids dangling at her sides, the fire steadily growing in the kiln.

The child dreamed from the backseat of the car. She dreamed of mountains that were slate-colored, maroon, or white with snow. She dreamed of the sun on the snow, of following the path the light made up the mountain until she reached the sapphire of the sky. In the dream, as she walked, she could hear her mother calling her from the fruit orchard of her old home. She could smell bread baking and her senses started to battle for control. What should she follow? Her mother's voice? The scent of bread? Or the shimmering, dancing, light?

If I Were Salmon

I have decorated my desk area with pages ripped out of travel magazines. Coral reefs with bright orange sea horses, schools of silver fish, beautiful blue skies. Baobab trees in Africa, women with black clay pots balanced on their heads. A bamboo hut where a man hangs in a hammock, a lemur perched on a mangrove tree.

Mingled in with the exotic are the familiar: the clay out-croppings of the Colorado National Monument, where I hiked last December. The alluvial fan in Rocky Mountain National Park, where Lawn Lake Dam broke and killed two rangers the year we moved to the mountains from Iowa. A river running through Montana, where rainbow trout wait for me to learn a new trade, to cast my fly into the water, and take up the traditions that were passed down to me.

When we'd go fishing, on family vacations, my mother looked so lost sitting in the middle of the rented motorboats, the bright orange jacket belted tight around her waist. She was never relaxed like Dad was, his ankles propped on the lip of the boat. Her nervous eyes darted around at the fluid water as it lapped the aluminum sides. The changing, mercurial nature of it that she couldn't bring herself to trust.

But everything changes, I learned this early. She's the one who taught it to me, while remaining rigid herself. In fluidity, I find solace. In stagnation, suffocation. After too long in one place, I feel the invisible tugging in my center, the twitching in my hands and feet. It's time to go. And I picture my father looking at his watch.

No matter where we were: the library or Disneyland, Dad never allowed us to lose track of time. To linger in any one moment too long. And maybe my mother, maybe that's why she left him. Perhaps she found a moment all to herself, and it was a good one, so she allowed herself to stay. To capture all of its details, its every particle of promise. As I look at the whites of her eyes, all that I can see with her pupils glued to a TV screen, I think that maybe she's still there now. Maybe she's afraid if she leaves that moment, she'll never find another one that's quite as good again.

The family vacation is an odd American ritual. It's a highly elaborate process that involves weeks of planning and packing, days on the road, and hours of arguing all for a few calm moments of enjoyment. It's the taking of lives lived parallel to one another and forcing them to merge for a common goal: catch this fish, climb this trail, brave this rollercoaster, together. My sister, then a teenager, would pretend it was the worst punishment of her life to have to sit next to me in the car for eight to ten hours, but I knew she secretly enjoyed counting out the alphabet on license plates of fellow travelers and singing made up songs about lakes. The four of us in the interior of that car was the community she had defined herself by, the community we had all defined ourselves by, and we didn't yet know how to navigate any other way. My mother, on the other hand, was tugging at the strings. The rift between the actual and the ideal was getting wider and wider and would continue to until the gap was big enough for all of us to fall through.

I dream of deserts. Of Tibetan mountaintops. Of the interiors of rainforests, the air as thick as blood. I dream of lying on a beach in Greece, the white sand slowly settling in my skin, the rhythm of the waves causing my scattered thoughts to still. Of life on a boat, unmoored. In his memoir, Another Bullshit Night in Suck City, Nick Flynn writes: "When everything has proven tenuous one can either move toward permanence or move toward impermanence." He was living on a boat in Boston Harbor at the time. And it's easy for me to imagine myself next to him, grabbing the rough rope in my small, tough hands and casting it off into the water. Placing my palms on the stern and breathing in the salty air. Each breath measured, calm, settling me further into the notion of floating with no goal in sight.

When we weren't fishing, we were haunting the hotel swimming pools. My mother sat at the edge, dangling her legs into the cool, unnaturally blue water. I recall the overpowering scent of chlorine. Sometimes, she'd wade in up to her waist in her black skirted one-piece. She'd wade until the skirt floated gently on the water, but never farther, because she never learned to swim. Tells it as if she's not embarrassed, hides all traces of wistfulness in her voice. But I can still hear it, an undercurrent. While we laugh around the dinner table, she tells us how that boy threw her into Lake Manawa on Senior Skip Day. How she screamed and flailed her fists at the too-yielding surface of the water, tears streaming down her pale cheeks until someone yelled at her to *put your feet down*! - and she did. I can see her, standing, blushing, vigorously crossing her arms over her chest, shooting daggers from her eyes at the insolent young man. "I can't swim", she'd point out, instantly turning all blame, all fault in the situation, outwards away from herself. Something she still does to this day. Even now, as we laugh about it, I can see in her eyes that she didn't think it was funny at all, that she still doesn't think so now.

So she put me in swim lessons that I hated at age nine, and I glowered as the instructor held his firm arm underneath me, kicking my little legs for all I was worth, her image in my head the whole time. I didn't know these were the seeds of resentment, or when they began to be sown. I knew only that I didn't want to be responsible for doing what she could not. For keeping alive the fragments of dreams we had left from our idyllic life in Colorado, for I was the only fruit of that labor.

The child searched the new land for water. She searched for lakes with jagged peaks reflected in them. The child missed the darkness of original waters and she missed the way light inter-rupted it and fractured itself into a thousand rainbows. She searched, but she could only find a mud brown river carrying things that decay on a twisting path to the gulf.

The Girl With Impermeable Armor

Somewhere along the way, it's clear that I set myself apart from the rest of my family. They were responsible for the position I was in – my life was not my own. One Christmas among many, my sister and I sat at Mom's dining room table – the same one she's had since before I was born. On the wall are her curio and spoon collections, which hung behind us as I blew out the candle on my first birthday cake. This lack of evolution, it's been killing me.

    We look at photographs from the golden years of what used to be tradition: Mom and Dad carrying their presents in one tall stack out of the living room. Then it was Mom carrying her presents. And Dad carrying his presents. In separate houses. Now no one at all. Then there's me, in the purple snowsuit and the three sizes too big bright red goggles. My sister, in the ski lodge, drinking hot cocoa, getting boys' phone numbers. She pretended to hate the snow. She pretended to hate everything. I was the winter girl, snowmen in the yard, our parents gone out and Tina locked in her room, phone cord trailing out from under the door.

    I looked at my sister, searching for recognition. A cigarette hung from her mouth. I had quit a year prior. We look nothing alike. Her hair was dyed maroon, mine was dark as ever. She used to be the pretty one. The cheerleader. I wanted to be her, but she never knew it. She scrutinized my perfectly shaped ass as she walked by on her way to the kitchen.. "God you're so skinny," she said. Perfect is what she meant. If only she knew.

We have mixed drinks in the kitchen. Southern Comfort and a splash of cranberry juice. Mom's was just the opposite. Tina's somewhere in between. "So, girls…." We looked anywhere but at each other. I started thinking of triangles, how the third element always manages to upset the balance of duality. Mom. Tina. Amy. The third. In the other room, the baby was napping – my sister's, not her first one.

"Why ain't you got a boyfriend yet?" My sister asked me. She talks this way. Got her GED when she was twenty-nine. She has to hit the only way she knows how. And even though they all think I'm unflappable, I felt it, still feel it. I collect moments like those.

I ain't lookin', is what I want to say. Or, *maybe I'm into chicks*. But she wouldn't get it. And I love her too much. I'd feel the guilt for days. I'd sweat it out through my pores. I shrugged, chugged the drink. I over-exaggerated the sound of my satisfaction.

From where we sat, I could see the presents stacked under the tree in the living room. Their shiny paper, some gold curling ribbon. The mismatched decorations on the tree. Somewhere in that pile were the misshapen gifts that I brought. Probably hiding in the middle, toward the trunk. Somewhere in that pile was the blanket I bought for the baby I still didn't believe would live.

The sound of us three women sipping our drinks was the loudest in the house at that moment. I wanted to be a child again, napping in the other room, like the baby who I still couldn't call by her name. I wanted to hold up my pain to the light like the injured finger my sister had slammed in the closet door when I was five, present it to Mom to kiss and make better. Instead we swallowed our pain in liquid form and looked anywhere but at each other, all of us listening hard for the small sounds an infant makes as she sighs and stirs slightly in sleep.

It's midnight. The wind is threatening to blow me away. A kid is missing from the college I attend. A child, really. I could have known him, but I don't. The chill, it's getting to me, it's getting under my skin. Flash back to my mother turning to me, bewildered. "A forensic anthropologist? What does that mean?"

"It's alright, Mom," I say. "God just gave her body back to the land. She's in the river now, and the trees. And soon she'll be in the sky." Her fingers tighten and weld to mine, and we go and sit with my sister. The detective has tried to explain to my mother that they can't show her the body of my niece. But natural processes don't make sense to mothers – only to scientists like me. I take a deep breath and pull it way down to the bottom of the newly hollowed cavity in my chest. My mother's eyes are all over the room – on the ceiling, the floor, at me. In fact, all eyes in the room seem to be upon me. Reverting to instinct, to the language of the body, I grip her hand tighter in mine. I try to send the message through my fingertips, to make her understand. But she only cries harder in frustration.

On the other side of me, on the couch, my sister is a statue. My sister the gossip queen, the girl who led cheers and smacked her gum and did her best Cyndi Lauper in the living room. In my mind, because of some biblical reference imprinted long ago, I am convinced she has turned to stone, and if she speaks will crumble into sand. I have been to both coasts and across an ocean, but I have never seen distances such as these. Still, I am doing the best I can to cross them. At night, when everyone is gone the three of us, the three birthstones on my mother's ring finger, huddle together in the same bed, under the same comforter, and I let them cry me to sleep.

I only saw her, held her, once. I drove the two hours to my mother's home on a cold January morning, just before the start of term. We stayed huddled inside the house, my mother, Madison and I. We were the designated babysitters while my sister was at work. She was just a few weeks old then and the first grandchild in the family. Nine pounds of sweet soft skin. Her blue eyes were alert and rolling around the room, one of them a little lazy, giving her a dazed look of wonder. Mom would prop Madison on her forearm, her little legs dangling over the crook of Mom's elbow and they'd do what we called "Grandma's swing." Madison would rise a few inches into the air and the smile would come, the small squeal of delight.

When I laid her down for a nap, a little later, I stretched out next to her on the bed, brushed my lips across her flushed cheek. I could smell my sister's milk still on her face: pungent, but sweet. In a soft voice I laid out our plans for the coming years: the trip to the zoo, the bedroom I'd do up for her in my house. How I'd buy her a plane ticket to come and visit me, because even then I knew I was already on my way out of this place. I just didn't know she was, too. That her father, who grew up broken and abused, was going to break and abuse his daughter, too.

A few weeks later: her funeral. In the sky, the clouds move like time-lapse photography. We are an amoeba of dark cloth: slacks static-clinging to themselves at the crease, pantyhose bunching up around knees. From all over the state, we have gathered like crows to stare at a white casket the size of a microwave, empty inside. A secret we kept from my sister. It was winter, and the animals were hungry. All that was left was a bit of bone. A remnant of a child who had appeared and disappeared so quickly it is sometimes hard to believe she were real at all.

In the parking lot, the chattering of teeth and words is carried away by the strong February breeze. My frozen fingers wind around a thin ribbon of white, the string to a pink balloon that slides through my thumb and forefinger as I walk out onto the icy church driveway, one of hundreds floating up into the gray February sky.

The third drink went down smoother than the first. We were down to the dregs of the bottle. Mom was in her bedroom, stroking the new baby's cheek. Tina and I were still looking at old photographs. Our baby photos. And the photo of the one we lost, the one her unfortunate choice in men took from us.

I tried to be stoic: the webbing between our fingers as we gripped hands, and her tears soaked once more into my sweater, mixed with an earlier stain: her new child's drooled milk. I was silent, but I wanted to say, Part of all of us died that day. I wanted to tell her how I sometimes forget to breathe, when I think of that tiny triangular wedge of bone from my niece's skull that was all we were able to bury. Shaken until she was blue. Left alone out in the cold. I wanted to tell my sister how I sometimes dream of her kneeling in sweats by the snow, wiping Madison's headstone clean with her stubby fingers, nails bitten to the quick.

Look outside, Tina. The frost is forming on the windows. Look at the pictures. Remember building that snow fort, at our old Colorado home? We were winter girls once. Always. Remember? We built those shelters and took refuge in them together.

In the New Place, the child never forced her mother to carry all of the burdens that a mother must carry alone. The child lifted them from her when her mother was preoccupied with the laundry or the dusting. It was as easy as sneaking salami from the refrigerator late at night. Her mother would knot her sweater belt tighter around her waist and shiver as if there were a chill in the air. But she did not notice the child's eyes growing steadily darker. Her small shoulders straining under the weight of the burdens she took on without anyone asking her to.

How to Become Ash?

We are disconnected, my family and I, my people and I, as this narrative is disconnected. We are dust and stone, sand and bone – particles loosely circling each other in weakly magnetic fields. So how to forge a family amidst all these tenuous connections? I am one-quarter Irish, yet the only one in my family who seems to have retained their ability for storytelling. Thus I know little of my parents' childhood, or of their life before me. I don't even know very much of their life after me. My grandfathers both died before I was born, and they remain as ghosts, photos I've seen once or twice stuffed in the back of a dusty album. So I set out to find out who these enigmas were, these ancestors, these bits of wisdom coded and hidden in my blood.

As a start, I asked both of my parents to tell me about the grandfathers I never knew. They became my rememberers, letting me in on pieces of history that should have been mine but were denied to me by fate and circumstance – and as it turns out, by parts of our national history that intervened on the trajectories of many American families.

His friends called him 'H'. William Harold Samuel Clark. My paternal grandfather: born 1907, died 1977, 3 years before I was born. He grew up in Missouri, had an 8th grade education, and then worked road construction and married Lucille in 1929. He would have been 22 and she 19. My father says that they were very happy together. They lived for a while, together with their 3 children and grandpa's brother, his wife, and their four children in a two room log cabin while Grandpa helped build the U.S. Army training base Fort Leonard Wood, near Rolla, Missouri, where my father would go on to live for a few years in his sixties. This enabled me to start college in Missouri, and allow for the circumstances that would eventually haunt me there.

My father says that my grandfather was "the most honest man I ever knew". He loved to play baseball with his children, and card and board games with family and friends. "He could look at a side of a hill and tell you how many yards of dirt you could take off it to build a road." I imagine he was a kind, helpful, and loving man. A bit of a dreamer, like his youngest son.

    Like my father, he always regretted not being able to fight in the war of his times. He was ineligible for the service, having had flat feet, a hernia, and 3 children at home. But war did not escape him. After working construction crew on Army training bases, he helped to build one of the first nuclear plants in Hanover, Maryland. My father suspects that that particular job is what planted the seeds of lung cancer that would kill my grandfather at a spry 70, making sure I never met him, and a good 15 years before the ages at which everyone else in his family had died. The Clarks have a gene for longevity that was tainted in my grandfather, it seems. Yet it makes me hopeful that my father, at 72, will live to tell me many more tales of him.

My maternal grandfather, who also perished this earth before I entered it, was Frances Waugh, called 'Frank.' His widow, my grandmother, tells me that he could tell where a vehicle had been from the dirt that was left on the tires. A sheriff's deputy, he was often a boon to my mother's teenage existence. She'd come home from a date and he'd prod her: "You've been driving through Fairmount Park, haven't you?"

    Fairmount Park still exists in Council Bluffs, Iowa, where I grew up. There are winding roads that lead through its moderate hills, one in particular that leads to an overlook where teenagers in the fifties and sixties would park their cars and 'neck.' My mother's own neck, turning, I'm sure, a bright flushed pink when she'd come home from these outings only to have her law enforcement father inspect the dirt residue on her car. But I was also told a story about how my grandfather took my mother out on a different kind of date: just the two of them, father and daughter, the middle child of five who was often overlooked. I am told they went shopping for a present for my grandmother, his wife, her mother. That they stopped for dinner and ice cream after at some soda fountain long torn down, and my mother got to inhabit the spotlight for once in her life, having had all of her father's attention, a place she would never get to inhabit again.

Memory is notoriously unreliable and exists in fragments. So I have to seek out those who still remember my family and pull out the fragments like bits of shattered glass, piecing them together into a mosaic that will become my history, my background, a place to move forward from. I was in a car accident in August of 2007. Returning home from a backpacking trip in Wyoming, I was traveling the last stretch of interstate between Des Moines and Ames, Iowa, where I lived. I had approximately 20 miles to go when a car sideswiped me, and I overcorrected and went in the ditch. I would have rolled to a stop, eventually, but for an underpass that happened to be coming up; so instead I hit a guardrail nearly head-on at sixty-some miles an hour. I broke the driver's side window with my head, and for two years afterward I found pieces of safety glass working their way out, reminders that past traumas are always present, that past histories shape our future.

At seventeen, I drove down to Missouri, toward my future, in the middle of a heat wave. Ninety-five degrees in the shade, one hundred percent humidity. No elevators or air conditioning were present to aid us in moving my belongings to the fourth floor of the dormitory. Sweat pooled in the small of my back. Andy, a friend from a summer job, had come along to help my parents and I carry boxes. I smiled at him over my shoulder as I set down an armful of bedding on my new mattress that nestled in a metal frame attached to the wall. It was a tense smile, a forced smile. I had never seen such close quarters.

In 1998, Maryville, Missouri had seven bars, a Wal-mart, and a Hardees that never closed. The town had no bookstore or library to speak of. No coffee shop to read my poems at. Andy stayed for a couple of days after my initial move, and we slept in a hotel room with much welcome air conditioning. I was glad of his company. We were friends of convenience, and sometimes more than, and I welcomed his company to ease me into my new state. I avoided my roommate, my room, until he left, but then I embraced the newness with fever pitch. This was my adult life, out from under the pressure of thumbs. This fresh, fiery hell was my own.

The August days grew longer, and then Andy suddenly showed up in town again to tell me he'd decided to join me at college. Why not? I wanted a clean break, but I didn't know how to say so. His room was across campus; not far enough.
I tried to avoid him, but he needed to talk. Let me into his room, locked the door. A Confederate flag hung on the wall over a hat rack above his roommate's bed.

"This is important," he'd say. "I don't want him to interrupt."

Important: carrying or possessing weight or consequence. Important: bearing on; forcible; driving. His lean frame pressing me into the same worn mattress. His thumb and forefinger encircling my left wrist, pinning it. His blue and green plaid sheets with my blood on them.

1998. Ten years since I was led from my home in the mountains. Fifty-odd years since my grandfather's family had left this state for more fertile ground. Three months after my father had decided, after only one year, to leave it, too.

Led by my mother's hand to the car that would take me there. Led by Andy's hand to his room. Drowning in his fluids and mine, I was further from any kind of home than I had ever been. I had moved to Missouri to find a new place to belong – but it used me, spit me out. The heat continued to rise. I was sweat and skin. Nothing more.

There is no nuclear power plant in Hanover, Maryland. My original deduction when my father said Hanover, Washington was that he was referring to our nation's capital. I now know that the project that may have killed my grandfather was located in Hanford, Washington in the Pacific Northwest, another place I would eventually call home. The site was located along the Columbia River, where I have swam and kayaked, and was established as part of the Manhattan Project. It was home to the 'B-reactor,' the first full-scale plutonium production reactor in the world. Plutonium from Hanford was used in the first nuclear bomb, tested at Trinity, and used in 'Fat Man,' which detonated over Nagasaki, Japan on August 9, 1945. There is a photo in the wikipedia entry of workers building the face of this 'B-reactor.' One of them may have been my grandfather, who his friends called 'H.'

In 1943, when Hanford Engineer Works broke ground, my father would have been 5 years old. I imagine, then, that Lucille and the children were left at home in Iowa or Missouri, while H went to stay in the construction camp with 50,000 other workers. It was said, however, that fewer than one percent of these workers actually knew what the fruits of their labors would be. The Manhattan project was still quite classified until the very public bombing of Hiroshima, which someone had to explain. 'H', my grandfather, was likely one of those fewer than one percent. Scanning the dirt mounds near his temporary surroundings, imagining the roads that would lead him back home.

Grandpa Frank wasn't always in law enforcement; he entered it late in life. Before that he drove buses and trucks, and worked as a mechanic in a garage he owned with his brother. My mother says he dreamed of going into the FBI, but lacked the education. Still, it seems to me enough of a feat for a laborer to make it into even local law enforcement, and it's a story I have yet to uncover from the memories of my rememberers.

I have his belt buckle, but no photographs. I have a vague idea of what he looked like. My mother, his own daughter, had to consult with others to paint a picture of him for me with words – a collective of words and stories pieced together from the memories of more than one person who knew him. It is interesting what survives: one man's dream, another man's downfall. A memory of an ice cream date, of sheets that may or may not have been plaid. A photograph that may or may not have my grandfather in it. An implication that this country fails to make good on the promises it makes to dreamers, time and time and time again.

Then we must sit at the fire and think about which song we will use to sing over the bones, which creation hymn, which re-creation hymn. And the truths we tell will make the song.

- Clarissa Pinkola Estes

PART II: BONES

The human body has 206. 22 are in the skull. In the forensic anthropology lab, we analyze the incomplete sets of them. Boiled bones, greasy bones, men's bones. Bones that tell stories. Porous from lack of calcium. Etched from a wielded knife. A healed collarbone. A broken toe. The unfused cranial sutures of a child.

But my bones tell none. Never fractured, still growing, still whole. They are dense and solid, covered in taut musculature, and refuse to yield despite the tests that I have put them through. Bones in alignment. Bones that ran a half marathon. Bones that climbed mountains. Bones that kept me standing when resolve failed the rest of me. Bones that said hello to new lands, new landscapes. Bones that waved goodbye.

When I write about the dead men in the forensic lab on the third floor of Curtiss Hall, my words read like this: "There is bone buildup on the right radial tuberosity, the glenoid cavity of the right scapula, on both tibiae near the knee joint and near the attachment of the Achilles' tendons, on both ulnae (but more so on the right), and ridging of the glenoid cavity on both scapulae. He appears to have been arthritic, and most likely right-handed. He probably did a high amount of physical labor."

I remain objective. I calculate standard deviations. I hold the heft of them in my hands. I wear gloves. I peer through the microscope. The holes in the bones are the holes in the stories of the bones. It's not easy as it looks on TV. I cannot tell how the men died, can tell only that they were men. I guess that one is white and find out he comes from Mexico. I measure his femur to estimate his height. My instructor gives me the answer key.

In Argentina, boxes of bones are lined up on shelves just waiting for someone to read their story, hoping that they get it right.

They are "the disappeared." Los Desaparecidos. The forensic team makes their best guesses. They write the stories of the bones in little boxes. They dream about skulls that once had faces, flesh that had bruises, feet that wore holes through their shoes. They wake to the sounds of bones ratting in their boxes, singing their bone-song, begging bury me, carry me home.

But where is home? Lineage is determined by mtDNA, taken from the marrow of the matrilineal line. Phylogeny is traced – branches sketched on paper – little leaves with surnames or species names scrawled in a cursive hand. Branches that stretch forever toward some distant "cradle of life." A grassy savannah. A torch-lit cave whose floor is littered with bones.

Is this how our ancestors lay? Bodies with backs to each other. Bones bent into questions.
    In Southern Nigeria they buried their dead like this: wives entombed alive next to their dead husbands. And I wonder if just one managed to claw her way out – struggle to the surface and leave tracks for some future archaeologist to find? Or, if women are innately satisfied with suffocation? (Fingers entwined in our husbands' long cold hands). Five generations of my family's females were born and have died in the same place - borders being something we lack knowledge of – still, I'd like to believe that our Ancestral Eve was the first cartographer - that she put miniscule maps in our cells so we would find our way back someday.

The child sat in the dirt at the bottom of the pueblo built into the hill. She watched her mother work pestel and mortar to make the evening's meal. Some of the flour escaped and settled on the floor – more fodder for the the grit and dust that was already in their skin, in the folds of their eyelids, in their hair. The child licked her lips and tasted the salt of the body's water. Remembered it, but could not place it.

mtDNA

The hip surgery went off without a hitch. It's the second one she's had replaced, and my mother claims to be ready to return to work after only two weeks, even though the doctor is 'making' her wait for six. She's still using a walker, and a raised plastic toilet seat, but other than being a little slow, she's 'fine'. And she's bored, having to refrain from the roles that have defined her for so many years: secretary, mother, housekeeper, cook. She is, at times, just as determined as I am and it's the first time I've realized this about her. Determined to keep her life on a steady and even path, while I am just as determined, it seems, to see how far I can let mine spin out of control.

This second time, I haven't sent any roses, not because I'm not thoughtful but because I can't bear to think of them wilting on the dining room table, my mother sitting there night after night watching them fade and refusing to throw them out until the petals start scattering themselves like a blanket over the faux wood. The way, it has always seemed to me, that she has always passively participated in life. For those are my dreams represented in the blooms of the roses. What part should she play in keeping them alive?

In addition to the hip replacements, my mother has been diagnosed with a terminal disease. Perhaps not terminal, per se, but incurable, at any rate. The disease is autoimmune, and also hereditary. It's called primary biliary cirrhosis, and it causes the body to attack the bile ducts of the liver. It will eventually kill whoever suffers from it, but it could take twenty or thirty years. My mother tells me this news nonchalantly over the phone. "No big deal, really," she says. "I just have to take a pill every day for the rest of my life."

For a while, I am able to follow her logic. After all, she's right. It could be worse. She doesn't have to lose any body parts, undergo radiation, lose her hair. She doesn't have to get hooked up to dialysis machines or endure any more surgeries. This danger, it isn't of the clear and present kind, so why worry?

And yet – these are the ties that bind us. I sit here and sip a beer, wondering if my own liver will suffer the same fate - though I'm told drinking plays no part in the process of this particular disease. But these are the ways in which we know we share one another's blood. We are bound by our defects, by our shared medical histories, as much as by the natural selection that has kept us alive so far.

I still recall vividly the one and only time my mother slapped me across the face – although I can no longer remember what prompted it. We were in the front seat of the car, driving down Avenue D to some school event that I resented her attending with me. But I hadn't learned to drive, and so was dependent on her presence. I was sixteen and still finding my way – figuring out who I was in the space of the shadows of those who came before me. Diminutive in stature, like me, my mother's shadow was not very large, and I was the biggest thing in it, in her life. I was the sole representation of all of her aspirations. I balked at that pressure, I didn't want it. I lashed out. And once, only once – she lashed back at me.

When I visited her after the first surgery, I had bought a dozen roses on the way to her house. I knew they were her favorite flower, but I had never asked her why – in my own opinion, classic was boring, and I was so busy separating my own identity, still, from the tangled DNA of my heredity, that I never explored my mother's reasons for anything.

She led me to the bathroom where we laughed at the giant plastic seat perched on top of the low toilet. And then to her same small bedroom, arranged the same way it always had been, where she showed me the devices used to pull on the stretchy socks that would keep her blood from clotting. She demonstrated the exercises that the doctor had asked her to do and then we walked back into the living room, perched on the edge of the couch like birds, and reenacted some instinctive ritual: an intricate pattern of alternating gestures toward and away from one another, and seemingly born at the edge of time.

A Native author, Louise Erdrich, writes: "In our own beginnings, we are formed out of the body's interior landscape. For a short while, our mother's bodies are the boundaries and personal geography which are all that we know of the world." I have a fascination with the concept of landscape: how we are defined by it and yet also defined in spite of it. I am one who believes that home is where you make it, but also that there are forces stronger than our own free will, the connection to our mothers being one of them.

Which leads me to ask the question: what is my mother's landscape? Suddenly, when I try to pin her down, I have no idea who she is other than a constant, sometimes nagging presence. A chest to bury my head in. Fingers stroking my hair back at the temples at night.

Some months after the surgery, I phone my mother frantically at 8 o'clock in the morning. She's been at work for an hour, but usually at this time she is at her desk flooding my inbox with forwards. This time, I think I'm on to something she hasn't seen yet, but I'm wrong.

"Mom!" I nearly shout. "Check your email. You have to see this lady sing."

Silence on the line for a few seconds as she clicks the link and then I can envision her smile on the other line as she realizes she's one up on me this time. Her whole office had already gathered around the screen the day before to watch it.

I'm sure by now that all of us in America have seen the unflattering yellow lace dress, the eyebrows thick as my thumb, and, sorry Susan, the ample hips that the "cheeky" Scottish woman is wont to wiggle around. And I'm sure, also, that many of us have found ourselves bringing a forefinger to the inner tear duct of an eye, suddenly finding something in it.

I grew up loving theater and musicals, and Les Miserables was always a favorite – but it doesn't explain the inexplicable emotional reaction I felt when watching Susan Boyle sing. Or the way she had touched so many of us, internationally, in such a short period of time. So what gives?

I have moved back to Iowa, the state I was raised in, four times now. Which means I've moved away four times as well. Each time I left I thought would be the last, and each return I viewed as temporary. But as I prepared to enter my thirties, I thought that this time I was home to stay.

And what does any of this have to do with a woman from a small village in Scotland? Because listening to Susan Boyle somehow feels like coming home.

On the other end of the line, my mother tells me the stories of how her office mates reacted. She is telling a story that numerous citizens around the globe can relate to, because we've all watched the same thing. She's sharing a dream with me, finally, and with a whole community of others who have united in support of a woman who isn't even from ours. We've gathered around a screen not to watch a wall fall down or towers collapse into rubble, but to listen to hope in the form of a song rise out the mouth of a most unlikely source. Hope that defies bombs, and murdered babies, and prison terms, and terminal diseases.

Outside my apartment window, the sky flashes with the first lightning I've seen in awhile. During brief year that I lived in Portland, Oregon, the drizzle never stopped and the thunder never came. I didn't want to admit it, but I had missed my home. I missed the flatness, the way I could always see the storms coming from a distance and prepare to weather them. I missed the open spaces that we travel across to reach each other, over and over again.

Before the child was a child, the child was an egg. She was one among many, floating in a nutrient rich fluid, waiting to be chosen for her journey. She was not a she, but perhaps always destined to be. She was formless, waiting to become form.

Mitochondrial Eve

I have five sisters, yet I was raised as an only child for the most part, and so never learned the ways in which women relate to each other until well into my adult life. Five sisters by my father, that is, all of whom resented the affection he showered on me, his baby, his last child born when he was forty-two. Strange to have so many siblings and grow up with imaginary friends – the favorite of which I didn't give up until I was nearly twelve years old. My other friends were characters in books, or characters in stories I wrote – the imaginary friend turned concrete via pencil on page. For they were more real to me than my actual family ever was. I understood only separation, isolation, the ways in which we break each others hearts, instead of the ways in which we are connected and come together bound by bonds of blood, yes, but also of shared community and shared history.

I have five sisters, and I don't know when any of their birthdays are except the one who is also my mother's daughter, the one I lived with for half of my life. The other four remain vague entities, figures huddled together and whispering at a wedding, faces in shadow and tears at a funeral. I don't know how they look when they wake in the morning, or just before they go to bed. I don't know their favorite colors, songs, television shows, or the stories of their heartbreaks. I have five sisters born sometime before my time, circling my periphery like stars.

The number five represents the pentacle – which, when pointed in the proper direction, is representative of the species of man. Four elements united by the spirit of mankind in a star-like web of five. Five daughters makes a complete set; count them off on five fingers. But six – six reaches beyond five to what some call the perfect number, a continuous curve without angle, without line, reaching towards infinity. I have five sisters. My father has six daughters. We are connected by numbers, if nothing else.

Two of my sisters have two sons and one daughter, and another has two sons and two daughters. One of them has just two daughters, and another has no children of her own at all. Three of their sons were born before I was, and so we were raised as cousins, even though this isn't true. One of their daughters I taught how to read when she was seven and the school system had failed to teach her. Now this daughter is a successful nurse at twenty years old, ten years my junior, with a pension plan and a better career than I will probably ever have. Some of their sons and daughters now have children of their own. Which means that some of my sisters are also mothers and also grandmothers, yet we are all our father's daughters and we are defined and not defined by these roles.

I have always enjoyed the fable about the six swans. The story goes that a great king had seven children from his first marriage: six sons and a daughter. He remarried, and the token evil stepmother resented the children and turned them into swans, all accept the lone daughter who was hiding in the forest cottage and so escaped the curse. This left the little girl alone to find a way to turn the birds back into her brothers, and to do this she must remain mute and isolated, knitting sweaters for them that would lift the curse and return her family to her.

And so it is that I sometimes think of my brother and sisters in this way – as birds long flown away. And my family as one that is cursed by the things that keep us from each other – time, distance, heartbreak. It is up to me to find the threads of story and weave them together like a shirt so that we might be united once more.

From the vantage point of a waiting star, the child looked down upon what would be her new home, her new family. She saw the mother and the little girl, and the golden retriever called Rocky. She saw the father reading his book in front of the television. She watched them eat dinner together and tuck each other in. She tried to imagine this concept called 'family,' but couldn't quite make it take shape.

Standard Deviations

Mom has just carved the turkey and my sister has just lowered her awkward pregnant body onto a chair at the dining room table when the phone rings. I am in the kitchen, licking the cranberry sauce off of my index finger, which I have just removed from the circle of sticky gelatin. But I still manage to get to the phone first. The familiar recording reaches my ear. Will you accept the charges? I hang up quickly, before Mom can get suspicious, but she's already eyeing me.

Tina chimes in first. "Who was that? Your boyfriend?"

I roll my eyes. We're too old for these games.

"Tina," I say, "he'd call my cell phone." That is, if I had a boyfriend. "It was no one. Telemarketers." But I was always a terrible liar.

Mom sets the large serrated blade down on the platter next to the turkey. She stares at me. "It was him again, wasn't it? I told you he tried to call the other day, before you got here. Would you please write him and÷÷/.; tell him you don't want to talk to him? Tell him to leave us alone."

I want to explain to her, again, how I threw all the letters away three years ago when I moved back to Iowa. Remind her that she threw away the ones that came to her house since. Instead I reassure her.

"Mom, I'll contact him somehow, ok? I'm looking into it."

The fingers of my right hand are still sticky with cranberry. Bits of red have appeared on the white handset of Mom's cordless. I see them there while I try to look anywhere but into her eyes. I have yet to shoulder this burden. I've only been adjusting the weight of it all these years.

The "family" called him Loki. In Norse mythology he is the trickster, the shape changer, the killer of Balder, the god of light. Yet he is also known as the one who crosses boundaries, sometimes even becomes the boundary himself. He is often depicted as the misunderstood God, synonymous with Anansi, the spider of West African lore. He has the ability to simultaneously charm and repulse everyone he comes in contact with.

Brian wasn't my boyfriend. He was my guardian, my protector, the one whose back I followed through the dark adolescent nights. He went to college with my high school boyfriend, Jeff. There was a group of them that bonded like family. And when Jeff moved away, I graduated from high school and drove myself to Missouri to take his place. His family became my family. Welcome, my daughter, they told me. Hello, little sister, they said.

There were six of us that became inseparable. Mara, George, Peter, Tony, Brian…Amy. And Winston, the storyteller, who occasionally wandered in our midst. We needed his voice to guide us through the night. The five of them did anyway. While the dice rolled, I sat at the corner of the table and watched. I admired the way Brian mediated the conflicts in the game. I followed every move of the thief he chose as his character in Dungeons and Dragons. And after a while, I studied how the grins started at the corners of his mouth and slowly crept upwards until one side would shoot up faster than the other and send a glint into his blue eyes.

Fast forward to Tony's apartment, some night when we weren't playing games. Not the kind with books and rules and eight-sided dice anyway. Perhaps we were playing "asshole" or some other college drinking game. We were flightless birds, testing our wings. Tony was in his kitchen, sitting in the dark on a metal folding chair. When I stepped into the room to pour another Jack and Coke he held a red candle in his right hand and dripped the wax onto the underside of his left forearm. His jaw was set. The muscles in his cheek barely twitched. His eyes were unfocused. I came and went undetected.

When I returned with my Jack and Coke to the living room, I stood with my back to the wall and then slid down, stared into the dark liquid. Mara, the only person I've ever known to be allergic to alcohol, sat cross legged on the floor not far from me, glaring at her too-drunk boyfriend where he lay with his long head of hair in her lap. Winston was playing video games. Brian was on the porch with Peter smoking a joint. I can't tell you about last week, but this day stays with me.

When my trickster came inside, I looked up at him. His eyes searched my face. I'd been avoiding them all night. And now, I knew: He knew that I knew. He was ashamed. I glanced away, but he pulled the drink from my hands, dumped it out in the kitchen. I followed him out the door while Tony grinned strangely at us, the wax having cooled into a dull sheen on his arm.

It was a short walk back to campus, but Brian found a back way to make it longer. If I returned to that town, I'm sure I couldn't retrace it. I seem to remember brick and vine, and large looming shadows. I remember reaching the dock at the small pond, hanging our feet over the edge of it. The small pool of light on the murky green water, my boots threatening to pull my small body down into it.

Brian's eyes were sodden with tears. They were shape changer's eyes. Swimming in and out of focus. Changing colors from blue to green to grey. He choked up words, spit them out like hairballs. I tried not to look, to stare straight ahead. I tried to deny the natural fact of him, visceral, in my periphery. I reached out and placed a hand awkwardly on his back. I could measure the space to reach across, but I could not provide absolution. We slept apart that night, and I tried to reach him in dreams.

Fast forward to two poor girls sitting on a picnic bench on the sloped hill behind the dormitories. Staring through blurred eyes at the field where we played intramural soccer. Their red hair bright in the early morning sun, their hands clasped like sisters. They were fellow freshmen from my dormitory floor. I had drawn them into the sordid web.

Across the bench from them my hands were folded in my lap for I was no longer one of them. I had known what had happened before the arrests were made. I had introduced them to killers.

Yet we stuck together for a little while. We snuck around the dormitories like thieves, pulling things from the boys' rooms before the cops could get them. The books on role-playing, the vampire movies, any music that might prove questionable. We wanted to spare the two boys who hadn't pulled the trigger. From the media, from any added weight. And of course, we were mostly protecting ourselves. Eighteen and fresh in the world, what else was there to do?

The child moved through the world as if it were made of water. She took note of the pockets of resistance, and the air currents that made her float. She sometimes forgot that she could not breathe underwater, swallowed the whole lot of it, let the darkness take her until muscle memory took over and saved her from sinking clean away.

Los Desaparecidos

One: Melissa

When I was five, I lived across the street from a girl called Melissa. Her grandfather, Earl, was a holocaust survivor, blue-ink numbers etched in his skin. His wife, Edie, cooked us artichoke hearts, soaked in butter. We lived as sisters, inseperable. We pricked our tiny fingers with a needle and let them bleed together, held together with a band-aid for the magic five minutes. Blood sisters. We giggled. Forever. Earl looked on, all smiles.

How does a young life know how to anticipate disappearances? I had lived with a ghost my whole life. A stillborn baby, Jennifer, who had blue eyes and a shock of black hair. Or so she lives in my memory. All I know for sure is that I knew of her, my ghost sister, since I was cognizant of such things. She haunted our house, she haunted my dreams, and perhaps I even attached to Melissa to replace her.

But Jennifer was not someone I had lost. She was disappeared from the world, but not from my life, for she had never existed as flesh and blood within it. And so Melissa became the first. After the move to Iowa, we wrote letters for years, and visited each other once when we were thirteen – in some Colorado hotel that our parents brought us to. Lipstick on our faces. Rouge on our cheeks. Budding women trying to recall a childhood already long gone. And soon after, my best friend, my sister, faded away onto a path all her own. Her absence spread in my heart like the ink in her grandfather's skin.

Two: Nikita

Mother insisted that we call her "Princess," because Nikita was too long and too hard to say. She was afraid she'd look silly calling out that strange Russian name up and down the street. But she was *my* dog, and Nikita was her name. When we first brought her home she lived in a box in the living room, yelping through the night, missing her mother, peeing on my Pound

Puppies sleeping bag. Daytime, she'd hide under the microwave cart in the kitchen, watching my mother's feet pace back and forth across the floor.

In December, when she was a few months old, she got to experience her first Christmas. She tore into the wrapping paper with her teeth. And just like a child, she was more thrilled by the process of revealing than the actuality of what was inside. My step-father had received a new set of barbells, and because Nikita was a Siberian Husky, a "working dog," he attached one to her new blue harness with a piece of baling twine and laughed as she dragged it around the room.

When my parents went out, she'd watch in the window until their taillights disappeared and then jump onto the couch where they wouldn't allow her. And every night she slept in my bed, underneath the covers on her side, her head on the pillow next to mine; patiently waiting for me to wake up and take her for walks in a climate she was never meant for. Or tie her up to the chain in the yard because my parents were too cheap to put in a fence.

Each brushing I gave Nikita would yield a paper grocery sack full of hair. I remember wanting to weave a blanket out of it once but not knowing how. We had four good years together, or maybe it was three. It's been so long that the only thing I remember is the bite she inflicted on the stranger who tried to pull her off of our porch, and how it meant I had to learn, again, to say goodbye.

Three: Nicole
Seventh grade and a spitfire of brown curls and backwards caps. That was when I met Nicole, my difficult, lovingly strange friend. I remember her choking on a nacho, across the choir room, my breath catching in my throat as I ran to pat her on the back and her loud echoing laugh after the chip had been ejected, congealed cheese all over my shirt. The long drive to Lincoln late on a Friday night for food at the Rock and Roll Runza. Vanilla Cokes and French fries…a large sundae wheeled out by girls in roller skates. All for an hour of flirting with a man who

we always knew was gay, but she never gave up. And I "took one for the team," because I owed her.

Senior year she had driven me the long two hours to Maryville, Missouri, so I could meet with Brian and his friends behind my parents' backs. She lay in a borrowed bed in silence listening to us kiss, never having had a boyfriend of her own. And she was the one I went on senior graduation trip with down to Kansas City and St. Louis because we couldn't afford a plane to the beach. Her car radio was broken, so we had to sing an off-key rendition of "Date Rape" by Sublime the whole way down. Well, I was off key, Nicole had a beautiful voice. And she'd sing to me the songs from her favorite off-color, off-broadway musi-cals. The ones that only Nicole would seek out and find the sheet music for.

In St. Louis, the Geo Metro deathtrap died and her step dad came down with a trailer to haul our asses back home. And we abused the short-wave radio to its fullest extent. And I was sure, again, that we'd always be friends. And I was wrong this time, too. We went to college. Drifted into the eddies of our own struggles. Forgot how to reach for one another.

And now I can only think of her, in the crazy costumes she'd make for Japanese anime conventions. Her hair that was sometimes cornrowed, dyed pink, platinum blond. How she bubbled over with forceful opinions, sure she possessed the magic to bend the world to her will. How her own will defeated her in the end, abandoned her until all that was left was a shell of a self, lying in a white casket, her face made up darker than it ever was in life, looking older, smaller, and so far from peace that I could barely rest my eyes upon the scene.

In the New Place, the Child missed the landscapes provided by water. Missed rushing rivers and canyons, shorelines and arroyos, shallows and depths and currents that could carry her clean away. So she took solace in thunderstorms that rolled like dinosaurs over the prairie, counting the beats between thunder and lightning. She stood on the porch and watched the sky turn to yellow, clouds funneling into tornadoes that threatened to level everything in their wake.

Littered With Bones

The van arrives in Shell, Wyoming in the middle of the night and we tumble out – disoriented fugitives running from what promised to be a sticky and boring Midwestern summer. Blue beams from hastily grabbed headlamps shoot out into the air at myriad angles, illuminating the rotting wood of the longhouse we are to stay in, a screen door that has long given up attempts to be flush with its frame, a patch of sodden grass. A young man whose name I didn't catch, who we've awoken from slumber, starts grabbing items at random out of our trailer. The sleeping bags tucked under each of his arms could belong to the male students, for all he knows, but he isn't asking for confirmation. He marches into the empty cabin ahead of us, tosses our things on the dusty wood floor. Seven small single beds on aluminum frames inhabit the space: a couple of cheap dressers, a yellow swath of carpet meant to serve as a rug. He neglects to tell us other women are asleep just beyond one of the three doors in the room.

"All set?" he asks, without waiting for an answer.

A few of the women look around the room and their faces change with dawning familiarity. It seems the time for summer camp has arrived, though they thought they'd outgrown it years ago. I, on the other hand, was never sent to camp. There were three worlds I resided in: Mom's house, Dad's house, and the alternate reality in my head.

The other women giggle and unroll their sleeping bags. There is some bickering over who gets what bed, and which drawers in the two cheap chests we are to share. We left a group of writers, leaving for a month-long retreat. We have arrived in a fit of regression, tumbling backwards over the miles through time. To travel West, for me, has always been to move back, not forward, in time. I fall asleep dreaming of the mountains of my youth.

The first early morning, I crouch next to what is a river in this season – a stream in dry times, rocking on my hipbones as if they were haunches. The ground beneath the rubber soles of my sandals is muddy, the area patched with tall grasses and reeds. Even though I have spent the last few weeks anticipating being able to try my hand at fly-fishing, the current of Shell Creek is swift and brown and uninviting.

Instead, the stark gray driftwood catches my attention, the only thing not perceptively moving. I have always been fascinated by the color gray: its many hues, its many liminal states. And the notion of something that has been petrified and left behind. Petrified, but not afraid.

The pile of driftwood sits scattered, like littered bones - yet becomes solid as I try to place it within the rest of the landscape. The red clay outcroppings towering above me, across the creek. The damp soil my soles are sinking into. Like me, it does not fit. It is merely an observer, rocked back on its haunches, looking as if it might burst into flames at any second.

Two summers before, I was in the opposite of landscapes, across the cold Atlantic, on the wet, green island of Ireland. I'm at a pub, of course, when I hear a voice in my ear.

"Do you sing?" the Irishman asks.

My hair swings back and forth in response to the question. Incisors, crooked where a filling has chipped, are clamped down on my lower lip. If I speak, I'll give too much away. The older gentleman shakes his head in a universal language we all understand. He is the elder deploring the younger generation, wistful for moments long past.

In the next room, the 'D' string on a fiddle is being tuned. The dust of amber resin is being ground into the wood floor as toes tap in anticipation. A 'session' is about to commence – in the basement of the Comhaltas Ceoltoirí Eirann. The building houses meeting rooms and hotel rooms for traveling musicians, a gift and information shop, and of course, a pub in the basement with an attached ballroom for hosting ceilis. Here, a pint is always Guinness, always cold, and always drunk with a toast.

Over the din of strings being plucked and tuned, tin whistles navigating scales, a man's voice rings out. If slightly out of tune, he makes up for it with a tone pulled from deep in his diaphragm that reminds me of my father's bold baritone. The voice he was sure could charm the pants off of any woman, or little girl. *The pale moon was rising above the green mountain/ The sun was declining beneath the blue sea/ When I strayed with my love to the pure crystal fountain/ That stands in beautiful vale of Tralee.*

The gentleman with the questions, the one who assumed I belonged, joins in from somewhere behind me, and soon two thirds of the voices in the room have become one. My lips, however, are still pressed together, or nervously dragging off the filter of a Silk Cut. The stigma of the black sheep that I just can't seem to shake.

At the end of the song, glasses are raised, and we drink the dark liquid another inch down. The fiddlers are ready, bows start to spark, and it begins to matter less and less who is Irish in the room and who is not. I smile and control my face to make it seem as if I know the music, as if I've lived the history that created it. The older gentleman glances at me occasionally, this mysterious insolent youth with the Black Irish blood in her, the pale skin, the hazel eyes, the stubbornness. And I want to adopt a new story, any story but my own to tell him. Instead, I order a glass of whiskey and swallow. Bushmills, on the rocks. It numbs and soothes.

Here in Ireland, I am starting to feel the ashes of so much angst wash away with the rain. Twenty-three out of twenty-five days, it rains – but I don't mind. Our first Guinness in the country is met with wet hair and wet wool sweaters, stares and glares from the locals. I've trained for this. I gulp it down like a lady: in seven swigs flat.

Ever since we left Colorado, the concept of home has been somewhere where I am not. Some mythical place to return to or to arrive at - I have never really been sure which. Because Ireland was in my blood, then, it was easy to project "home" onto it. To walk the rain-soaked bricks with my head held high and meet people's eyes with a smile. Among strangers, I could inhabit the persona that I had invented, the girl who had evolved right alongside of them and knew this was where she belonged.

The room settles into the quiet buzz of conversation, punctured by the hearty Irish laugh. I'm still working my way through the pack of Silk Cuts, inching my way down the glass of whiskey. In Mircea Eliade's book, The Myth of the Eternal Return, he says "an object or an act becomes real only insofar as it imitates or repeats an archetype. Thus, reality is acquired solely through repetition or participation." If the woman-I-want-to-be is ever to achieve reality, I have to make her participate, make her sing. But I am saved from singing by the start of the ceili in the next room. A band is on stage, and folks are gathering at the perimeter of the room. Our group of ten settles themselves in chairs at the back.

In a ceili dance, an announcer stands near the musicians to announce the steps. Akin to square dancing or Scottish country dancing, couples form and make groups of four. The teens are nervous, but the adults are sure. Like the singing, this dance is tradition, and their feet have walked the path many times. I have taken fourteen years of dance classes in tap and jazz techniques – but none that involved any level of intimacy. My greatest routine was a solo one. So it must have been a glint of longing in my eye at the movement on the dusty hardwood floor that makes Zac, a classmate, grab my hand and lead me out. Unlike many places I have visited, the Irish are offended if you *don't* adopt their culture as your own, not if you do. The evening unfolds in a series of blurred images, my hair flying behind me, my hands in the hands of others.

Back in Wyoming, on our first free day we travel to Cody. I stand outside of a coffee shop, owned by a rock climber and his wife. I don't tell him that I belong to his tribe: that I'm a fellow climber. I don't tell him how I revel in the sense of accomplishment that comes with each hold I stick, knuckles locking in place, one step closer to finding the correct sequence to the top. I decide to phone an old friend from the mountaineering club who has just moved to Seattle. Both of us wanderers in strange cities. He tells me I would love it there. How the people there are faceted like jewels. How he wants to design a building for me. Each corner a quirk, each staircase an achievement.

Down the street, a German Shepherd barks before diving under a bench. A woman rides her bike, head thrown back into the wind. Dolly Parton's song "Jolene," blares from outdoor speakers. I lean back in my metal chair, take a long sip of espresso and tell him the coffee here is as good as any in the Northwest.

"I could stay here," I say. "Just leave everything behind…" A pause. "I'd send for the cats, of course."

I can hear him smiling on the other end; feel the tires of his old black Honda rolling down the cramped Seattle streets. In our separate states, all senses are engaged. Neurons, aided by coffee, fire more than they have in months. The invisible line crackles with possibilities.

The Smithsonian Institute's Natural History Museum dedicates a rather large wing to housing its gemstone collection. The Hope Diamond being, of course, the museum's prize asset. It spends all day inside its bullet-proof display case, twirling slowly before the crowd of onlookers like a ballerina in those music boxes mothers like to give to daughters. The hallways containing the rest of these precious stones, polished to perfection, are always thronging with visitors. Diamonds can be red, black, pink, blue, yellow, or white. Sapphires, my birthstone, which I had previously thought only had one hue, can actually be blue, pink, purple, yellow or green. They can also be deep red, in which case they are called a Ruby.

The most talented lapidaries in the world encase the gems in precious metal in every shade of platinum, silver, and gold. They have been cut to give off such sheen that any self-respecting girl would buckle at the knees upon viewing them.

When I visited the Smithsonian, I may have felt a twinge of jealousy or two, but for the most part, I wasn't interested. Instead, I lingered in the back hallways, where they keep the asteroids and moon rocks. The ones that brought back memories of primary school field trips to the planetarium. You're allowed to touch these. And I thought how if life ever existed on these neighboring celestial bodies, it flashed so briefly even the rock didn't have time to record it. At least, not the rocks that fell burning through our atmosphere. When I want to record a moment according to my sense of time, I write a poem. When the Earth wants to write a poem, it hardens into rock.

Out here in Wyoming, we kneel down in front of dinosaur tracks bigger than my father's palm. Evidence of tail drag runs between the three-toed impressions in the sandstone. A geologist, head of the camp we are staying at, shows us bulges on boulders that are bigger than my head. These, he says, are where the flat feet of the herbivores sank into the sodden soil. Where the earth decided to remember them, to allow them to say: *we were here.*

In Rising from the Plains, part of a quartet of nonfiction works exploring North American geology, John McPhee explores how each layer of rock tells a story. He follows geologists around, listens to their stories, then translates them into the written word.

I cannot look at a landscape, like a geologist, and see its history. In the Museum, I am most attracted to the uncut stones, the rough and random shapes of them. I am taken by the fact that no matter how intuitive I pretend I might be, I would never guess what dazzling possibilities lie inside them.

Back from Cody, we sit around the cabin while a thunderstorm rages outside. Tornadoes touch down ten miles away. Outside, the sheep from the neighboring ranch bleat like they are dying. I put on a CD to drown out the sound, but the first measure of music sends me spiraling back to that Saturday morning six weeks ago. Cross-legged on the black futon, in the living room of my friend Matt's minimalist Portland apartment. I am reading the poetry books his brother has checked out from the library, waiting for his presence in the white-walled room. When it comes, he is barefoot in sweatpants with a lazy half-smile. His eyes alert and engaged as he stretches his arms above his head and bends his yoga-toned body at the waist to place his palms flat on the floor. He tells me he hasn't slept so well in days.

 We got in well after four a.m. the night before, but I've been beyond boundaries of time since I arrived. Not since I visited Ireland has a place seemed so ethereal. Every front-yard is landscaped. Foliage hangs over the streets and sidewalks, green and alive. Even the air, cleansed daily with rainwater, is full of magic and possibility.

 He strides over to the record player, eager to share his recent finds. A male voice fills the room, tremulous and haunting. *Losing, it comes in a cold wave of guilt and shame all over me/ Child has arrived in the darkness, the hollow triumph of a tree.* I am close to tears. I gaze at his face and for the first time he doesn't look nervously away. But his arms are folded tightly across his chest and he is rocking slightly on his heels.

 "Let me show you the garden," he says and laughs. His mouth working a wad of gum. That distinctive quirk I remember.

 We step out onto a single square of sidewalk at the edge of a small area of mud and grass. No plots of squash grow here. No green beans, no lettuce, no fruit trees. Not even a picnic table adorns his tiny yard. But I slip my sandals off anyway and make tracks around the perimeter with the soles of my feet. "It's wonderful," I say.

 He stands in the doorway watching me, working his wad of gum.

 The song slowly fades, and I grow to inhabit my senses again. From the cabin, I can hear the sheep from the neighboring ranch crying. Maybe they feel displaced, too. Maybe they miss their mothers, their fathers, the pastures of their birth. They are recently shorn and red paint adorns their sides. Numbered just like the nursery rhyme. But I don't plan on counting them. I'll allow them that much dignity.

I walk down the road to Dirty Annie's, the local hangout that serves as café, grocery, souvenir shop and bar. All the local gossip transpires on the porch. The men wear Stetsons and chaps, Carhart jeans and spurs. Some sport handlebar mustaches. Art is made from pieces of old tack. Bits of dialog float through my ears. "Chasin' girls and drinkin' whiskey." "Purty good." "Dark-thirty." One man tells me he got his degree from HKU. "Hard Knocks University," he explains.

A black horse is tied to the post out front. Rain clouds threaten, but don't deliver. The old boards creak, the dust rises and settles like the tide. The bottomless cup of coffee is good and will sustain me through this lazy Sunday that drawls on in the way of the West. I am content to fade into the background of this quiet afternoon.

Quiet, that is, until the busload of tourists comes for food, buggy rides, homemade ice cream. They line up to have their pictures taken with a "real cowboy." From my perch on the porch, I try to suppress a bemused smile. Knowing all too well that I am just as much an outsider as they are.

In her essay "Writing in Wyoming," Annie Proulx says: "I have always been in an outsider's position – perhaps the natural stance of a writer, though the outsider's eye is common to all humans." In this instant, on the aging porch, it is easy for me to smile up at the proprietor and his wife. To nod my head knowingly at how the tourists have turned them into caricatures, how they have gotten a cheap show. But haven't I gotten it too? In Wyoming, Portland, Ireland - I have always been just passing through. The day is slipping away. And even though I inhabit the moment, nothing lasting will come of any of this.

Once, the Child believed that the children of earth first perched on waiting stars. When they were called: by desire or greed, love or grief – they rode a quick thread down down down like ethereal spiders – already wise, already knowing how to survive in the waiting womb.

Cartographers

My mother is having her second hip replaced. She has a little card she can carry in her wallet to hand to airport security – an explanation of the metal that now substitutes for bone in her body. She only travels when she has to, so it isn't a recurring ordeal. The occasional wedding or visit to my stepsister – a visit to her daughter if I ever manage to move away again. I've tried to convince her to accompany me on various half thought-out adventures but she always rejects the ideas before I even have a chance to flesh them out. I'd ask why, but it's pointless. She's my mother. Because she says so, will have to be enough.

Personally, I've always loved airports – loved them for being definitive of all the things that come between one moment and the next, for never really harboring great moments in and of themselves. They're uneventful places, really, when you think on it. Most of what we do in airports is wait. We pass the waiting in interesting ways: duty-free shopping, pretending to be interested in some sports game or some stranger's travels over beers. Occasionally, we actually are interested and a friendship is forged, or a character sketch to save for telling our friends later. But mostly, airports are simply that: ports of call, stripped of seaside romanticism and outfitted instead with strip malls, McDonalds, Starbucks, sports bars and newsstands. People sleeping stretched across uncomfortable plastic seats or leaning against concrete pillars, headphones jacked into a laptop, plugged in near the coffee-stained carpet at the bottom of the pole.

Usually, I'm one of the loners – I prefer to travel this way, it's true, but it's also true that in airports I somehow come to miss my mother.

My mother and stepfather have been together for fifteen years. They've taken one vacation: to the Black Hills, in South Dakota. One state away. They brought me back a shot glass, as if drinking is the only habit they know I have. I can only imagine how the trip really went. My stepdad wanting to try out some local biker bar, reminisce on his days of riding the Honda that sits at the side of our house. My mother pursing her lips and setting her jaw. Her eyes only daring to light up for a flicker of an instant as they stand in front of Mt. Rushmore. When I ask her about it, later, "It was so neat," is all she will say.

I offer to take her to London, but she doesn't want to go.

"Oh, that sounds nice." Her hand dipping absently into a bowl of popcorn.

"You'd like it, Mom. They drink lots of tea. And it's not Lipton. But you've got to get your passport, and it takes at least six weeks. That's why I'm telling you now. I've got to get the tickets while they're on sale, so make up your mind."

"Oh, honey, it's so great that you got to go to Ireland. None of the women in my family will ever get to do anything like that." Tears welling up in her eyes.

I don't know if she's crying at the tv screen, or if some part of her hears me. Maybe it's a combination of both. I want to buy the tickets, forge her signature, sneak her photo while she sleeps and pack her suitcase in the middle of the night. She's fifty-four, not too old for adventure. But I don't know how to get through.

"You know," she says, the husk of a kernel stuck to one of her teeth. "When do I get to see something you're writing? You were always such a good writer."

I dug out the notebooks from high school over Christmas. The poems about suicide, about different ways to die. The marginal scribbles about how much I hated her. The typical, teenage, apocalyptic bull. If she'd read them, I would've known. Would've seen it in the set of her jaw.

So I don't know what her statement speaks of. I've come to believe everything she says lately is arbitrary. A repetition of something she heard someone say, once.

"Yeah? Which poem did you like best, Mom?"

She swallows. Looks away from the screen. Takes a drink of her black tea, with a teaspoon of honey.

"Oh, Amy, I like them all. I couldn't choose." Her cheeks flushing a slightly darker shade of pink. Suddenly she turns toward me. "Did I tell you where Mary is going?"

Mary is our next-door neighbor. A widow who raised five children, one of them schizophrenic. Her daughter used to bring me clothes ten sizes too big, not able to fathom that they wouldn't fit me, not realizing she was twenty years older, a hundred pounds heavier. But Mary took care of her, up until last year, when her crazy but usually well-behaved daughter hit her over the head with the base of the telephone.

"No, mom. Where's she going?"

"Macchu Picchu. It's in Brazil, I think. With that group of lady friends. You know, they always travel together."

But I don't know. It's the first I've heard of such things. I knew her daughter worked for the airlines. Knew that we picked up her mail while she visited her grandkids in Texas. I know that Mary is at least ten years older than my mother. But I don't really keep in touch.

"Peru, mom. It's in Peru. I dated a guy from there once, remember?"

"Oh. Well, you know. Somewhere down there."

As if "down there" were only as far away as my private parts. As if it were just as exotic as that. I stuff some popcorn in my mouth to keep from shaking her. Glue my eyes to the pixels on her TV screen. The small squares of black that add up to make a pupil, the blue iris around it, the seemingly unending white.

I know the whites of my mother's eyes very well. From looking at her while she looks away at something else. On the TV, a man slaps a woman across the face. She falls to the floor, into that perfect pose: one elbow bent to hold herself up, hair across half of her face, her dress riding up, the top leg bent at the knee. A few drops of blood are oozing out of the corner of her lip.

"Not in front of the children," the woman says. Isn't

everything in front of "the children"? I want to think no one is this ignorant. I want to think that at least my mother is not.

I fight the urge to grab the remote and shut the damn thing off. Or better yet, to throw it out on the front lawn next to the waiting garbage. I want to know what image my mother's eyes will scan without the presence of a screen. I don't remember the last time I saw her engaged, animated, in love with a moment. I don't know if I've ever seen her that way.

I pluck at the fabric on the couch, annoyed that her eyes have barely scanned my face this whole conversation. "Mom, seriously, we could go. We'll get a hotel a block from Big Ben. You don't have speak another language. It's not that different. And it could change your life."

"What?" The woman on the screen is now meeting with her lawyer. He looks like an underwear model, of course. His hand rests on her knee as he talks, and I'm disgusted. But at least he's listening.

I can feel my jaw settling into place, the bone becoming denser, heavier, welding itself together. Inheritance is a tricky thing. I rarely look at my mother and recognize parts of myself, but as I sit here, fuming, I realize this habit is inherited from her. While studying Anthropology, I've learned that primates have a highly evolved sense of mimicry. In facilities around the country, chimps are being taught sign language. They share ninety-eight percent of our DNA. They wear diapers, are raised on bottles by researchers. Watching a video on this, once, I was haunted by their all too human eyes staring out at me from the screen. By their familiar looking thumbs tracing their jaw line in the sign language symbol that means "mother."

Biological or not, it seems, we can't help but want to be like them somehow. The mother figures. The matriarchs. Lipstick smeared on my cheek at three. Marching around the house in heels. The way I hold my hands laced behind my neck during tense moments at the movies. I can't escape it. I know parts of me are bound to reflect my mother's image. But no one can blame me for trying to make parts of her a little more like me.

We visit the land of our secret grandeur in fantasy or in books and movies, and on the road between these imaginings and the actual house where we must eat and sleep, to the degree that we are able, assemble a life from the usable fragments of each.

- Lewis Hyde, Trickster Makes This World

PART III: SUTURES

I worked at a sandwich shop to pay my way through college. I had just moved to a town in which I knew not a single person, saw the sign in the window, inquired, and was hired on the spot to start the next day. That sandwich shop was home for the next six years, while I struggled to complete my undergraduate education, to keep my head above water, to keep the pills out of my stomach and the razor blades away from my wrists – to find my way. When one's internal landscape is as tumultuous as the surface of Jupiter, you learn to find solace in consistency, in simple tasks. Mornings, I would stand against the bread oven's heat and place my palms against the glass and let the small heat sustain me.

One day a few years in, we were busy with a line out the door lunch rush and the knife in my hand slipped off the unyielding plastic of a gallon of mayonnaise and found its way to the bone of my left thumb. I had spent hours in the past barely daring to press hard enough to draw beads of blood, to slice careful lines in the skin of my forearm that I would hide with long sleeves but smile at when alone. Now – in less than a single second – skin, muscle, and tendon all gave way until the serrated edge finally found its match in bone.

    I didn't even look at it. Simply walked quickly to the nearest sink and turned it on, sticking the injury underneath. Four soaked dishrags later and my boss and I were on our way to the emergency room, where I held the wadded cloth around my thumb above my head hoping and not hoping for it to clot.

In the ER, my boss and I waited for not very long. We were fortunate to live in a small city where there is enough health care for everyone. The doctor injected a needle in my wound – and I'll never forget the way he moved it all around to spread the anesthetic – torturous and relieving in the same moment. The way I wanted to look and not look and was dizzy with the pure rush of life gushing out of my veins.

Life drains quickly. I remember watching a film over and over with my friend Nicole – the one who died from downing handfuls of sample antidepressants – in which a young man in Nazi Germany bleeds himself out into a tub with clawed feet, banned jazz tunes spinning on the turnstyle in the next room. I remember never understanding why the red wasn't deeper, dispersed in all that water. Or why, in the movies, they always let the tub overflow to stain the floor around it, one arm lolling lazily over the edge.

In real life, violence is more visceral. In a second, or less, a body is brutally scarred, the life leaves a baby, a woman loses her innocence forever. An old woman's face: simply gone. I don't mean to horrify you with these images. But they are what is true: as tangible as the glaciers melting, the plastic polluting the ocean, the spilled oil suffocating the pretty heron you were just pointing out overhead. Look up: look at him: long legs dangling, dragging behind, but not dragging him down: neck arched gracefully towards the endless blue of the sky.

The child sifted through the wreckage of her neighbor's homes after the tornadoes ravaged the New Place. Saw the mawing gaps in the ground where concrete foundations used to be. Picked up the fragments of lamps, ashtrays, broken photo frames, and took them with her to be glued back together.

Jupiter

In the nurse's aid class, we learn how to fold fitted sheets. How to make a bed with someone lying in it. How to slide the chamber pot gently underneath their private parts. We practice transferring each other from wheelchairs to hospital beds with thickly woven gait belts. We spoon feed each other like birds. We learn to place two fingers gently on the insides of wrists, and tune out everything else in the world except the bounding pulsation of another's heartbeat through their skin and the rise and fall of their chests in rhythm.

When I was young, I was obsessed with wearing watches, and with knowing the exact time. Down to the minute. But I had thrown mine out years ago in a fit of rebellion against the sense of control that had kept me reigned in too long, that had kept my tears lodged somewhere in my diaphragm, and in every unused crook and cranny of my inner landscape, bursting to be released.

But now, in nursing school, I am required to wear one at all times – to watch the second hand with precision for accurate diagnoses. A heartbeat too slow or too fast or too irregular could be the first sign of many a bodily breakdown. And recorded history is also important. A list of facts, leading up to, we hope, something definitive: recovery, diagnosis, death.

My patients are on the med-surg floor. Mostly middle-aged patrons of common routine surgeries such as the removal of gallbladders, the placement of pacemakers, the replacement of joints long worn out. But I have one that defies the predicted demographic: a young man in his early twenties with a punctured lung. He is Asian, quiet, pulled inward into his recovery. The recorded history does not tell the story of the 'accident,' only that it was one. I write down his urine output. I check it for blood. I place my fingers on the skin of his forearm and listen to the sounds of his one functional lung breathing. I never see anyone come to visit him, and there are no cards or flowers upon his table.

In Portland, flowers marked the graves of bicyclists who had been mown down in accidents. I passed these small memorials on morning runs, internalized the grief placed there. A friend of a friend of mine witnessed one such accident. Biking home herself, she saw a man down on the side of the road, blood leaking from under his crushed helmet, cars continuing to pass by. She knelt by him. Held his hand while they waited an eternity in minutes for the ambulance. Watched the life leave his eyes. Probably never forgot their hue.

It is as if, sometimes, the planet we inhabit is both our own and not our own – as alien at times as the gas clouds of Jupiter and its great, looming eye. Most of our encounters are with strangers. Most of our experiences are singular. Sniff a rose and try to describe it, truly, to someone else. Can you? And yet when we are down, we reach for each other. We listen for a heartbeat. We kneel down on the concrete on already tired knees and lift a stranger's body into our arms.

The Child sometimes remembers when time was not a thing that could be measured at all. When she could wish herself somewhere and arrive, across what they now call 'light years' of space. Before The Grounding, every possibility was possible – every cell had the potential to become dragonfly or human, light-being or climbing vine, sentient or at rest.

Careful Lines

He tells me he used to be an artist, a potter, and I can almost see his hands at the wheel: his palms moist with clay, his fingers wavering in a gentle dance. I love him for it, but I don't know where any of this will lead. Here in Oregon, everything seems possible, but almost nothing is actual. The firm soil of the trail in Macleay Park a mile from Matt's house. The moist moss. The oxygen-rich air.

On the record player Tom Waits is singing the blues. The turntable spins like a potter's wheel. The music molds my thoughts like his hands once molded clay. A million questions rise to the tip of my tongue but I stay silent. I want to know, though, the color of the clay, the shapes that emerged from long hours of passionate production. I want to know how the brain that once conceived of the slender neck of a vase now calculates for hours on end. Solves other people's problems instead of his own.

I look around the apartment at all of his functional furniture: the clean lines of the black couch perched on squat metal legs. The perfect right angles that every piece contains. Not a single round object adorns the room. Not even a clock on the wall or a curved vase with flowers in it to brighten the stark empty walls. The only circular items are the records, hidden inside their squares of cardboard protection. And the lonely black one spinning away as I sit and stare into space.

So come on and swallow me, don't follow me/ I'm trav'lin' alone/ Blue water's my daughter/ 'n I'm gonna skip like a stone...

In the kitchen, Matt is making pancakes. It seems to me a huge step for someone who once lived out of the bed of his truck. A whole summer spent in the back of a red Tacoma, sleeping on a shelf. This domestic side of him is one I haven't seen. The records only have two, but he has multitudes. And I wonder if, looking into the batter, he can already see the perfect round shape that will emerge – its slightly ruffled edges. If he can envision the thickness, the weight of it on his plate like I envision the shape of his stomach beneath his shirt and how it would feel so firm against the gentle slope of my own skin. And how his hands could mold me into the shape I know I can be, that I am struggling so hard to become. Could spin out a structure for the skin that waits for me to step into it.

    I hear a plate clink down and I rise, follow my nostrils towards the scent of blueberries and strong coffee. I sit down across from him, where he's already started eating, his eyes scanning the paper, and I pick up the white mug of fresh coffee, press it to my palms to let the warmth soak in. The cool northwest air blows in through the open windows, freshening, awakening the apartment. But I put the mug down after only one sip because I know there's only so much I can hold in my hands.

I was thirteen when I first visited the Atlantic. I stood on the shore in Camden, Maine, and watched the sun slowly burn off the field of fog that had descended during the night. My feet were rooted but a part of me dove into her gray waters and still lives there, exploring. There's a photo of my face, hair blown across my pale cheeks by the wind, a dead seal purple and bloated and rotting on the beach behind me as I squint at the lens, bits of sand lodged in my eyelashes.

    I had visions of the posters that hung on the beige walls of my biology classroom. Those metamorphosing forms in their slow struggle towards land. Standing there I felt something calling me back, something that still calls, the black water beckoning me to return to my first home.

    Shortly thereafter I decided I wanted to be a marine biol-ogist. I watched this PBS documentary on orcas until I'd memorized the narration. The gravelly voice rising and falling in rhythm with the black fins following the waves. That worn out video dad bought for me in the gift shop at Sea World. I wanted to run my fingers over the rubbery skin of a whale. I was sure I'd find answers there.

Matt leaves for work, but he's left me a set of keys. I'm free to come and go as if this place were my own. I spin the record again, and this time spin with it, barefoot on the hardwood floors. *The fog's lifting, the sand's shifting, and I'm drifting on out/ Old Captain Ahab ain't got nothin' on me now ...*

    I pull on shorts, a tank top, running shoes. I tie the two keys to the drawstring at my waist. I grab the maps from the coffee table where Matt left them for me last night, after leaning so close to show me the trail I could smell salvation on his skin. But it isn't mine to have. He found his own way, alone. Through his silent stares he's trying to tell me that I should do that, too.

    I strap a water bottle to my wrist and take off down the street. I pass the Patisserie he told me about, where the people "pretend they're European." And it's true that the patrons look relaxed and satisfied. Mugs of steaming lattes, the frosting on éclairs seeming to shine in the sun.

    I walk on past the park where I sat yesterday reading poetry. Where I watched the families with their children spread out on blankets. A man carried his injured young daughter from the car, her leg in a cast, while his wife carried the crutches. A small boy who had just emerged from the fountain, stood patiently while his mother undressed him and then shook the water onto her as if he were a dog – his bare bottom twisting while everyone laughed.

    I pass "For Rent" and "For Sale" signs. And the single vacant lot in the neighborhood. That small landscape of possibility. My mind latches onto the image of a house rising up from the embers of my life thus far and planting itself here. Of Matt in the kitchen making pancakes, of a small boy shaking his bottom while the record player spins and spins.

    But although it is my destiny to create endless narrations, I cannot make them come true. This naked toddler, I can give him a name. I can cull him from the park and keep him on a page. I can tousle his hair and smile at Matt and let the word "son" rise to my lips. But the image ends when the ink runs out. I cannot make any of it live. I can make up an ending to belie my beginnings, but as I try to reach it, the middle inevitably grows longer.

I am not a strong swimmer. I had the obligatory two years of lessons, and after that I went to the pool solely to splash and play around. My father lived in California, by the ocean, but he didn't own a boat. He's no sailor, and when he fished, it was always on the safety of a landlocked lake. Not even the rush of rivers caught his attention. But we went to the beach often, because that's what Californians did. The parents lay on the beach with books or lovers and the children ran headlong into the water, throwing their small bodies into the force of the waves, relaxing as the water carried them home.

But I always had a different sense of it all. I'd beg to go when it was cloudy, when the crowds were thin or nonexistent. I'd wander along the shore, letting the foam settle over my toes, and stand there entranced. I'd imagine my heart beating in some primal rhythm with the tides, imagine it speaking to me in a language I knew but could not, can not articulate.

My stepmother, who also has a great affinity with the ocean, must have thought I wasn't enjoying myself. I must have looked so sullen, so lonely, wandering along the waterline, stopping occasionally to examine a shell or small crab. In reality, though, I was listening. I was trying to tune into a frequency I had never heard but knew, instinctively, was there. The waves did not want to push my small body gently toward shore, I knew. "The pull of the tides," that's what I'd heard men say. "The Stygian sea," I'd read. Those waves, they wanted to pull me, all of us, home. They wanted to bring us closer to the center we have come so far from, now.

When I reach the park, I check the map at the entrance to make sure I have come to the right trail. The Wildwood Trail stretches 27 miles throughout Macleay and Forest Parks, winds through the hillsides in the heart of the city. At the top of one switch-backed section of the trail is the Pittock Mansion. A mansion with miles of old-growth forest as its former residents' backyard. But no one resides there now. It is a tourist attraction, a façade. Just like these words.

My feet are hitting the ground but I detect no rhythm in the sound. I focus instead on my breath, on keeping my mouth closed as long as possible, nostrils flaring to their limits. I reach an old stone house and slow. The antithesis of the Pittock Mansion. This "house" is one wall of an A-frame, built of mortared gray stone. Moss-covered stairs lead up to a landing. Whether anyone ever lived here, or if this too, is for tourists, I can't say. I walk around in it, peer through the arched window, and then continue on. But I never make it to the Mansion. I left the map at home, and when I finally think I've reached it, I end up staring instead at a housing addition, some condos that all look the same.

Matt laughs when I tell him I couldn't find the Mansion. The biggest house in the hills. But then again one can't see over the trees. We climb into the Tacoma and he drives me up there. Braces his truck carefully against a guardrail because the emergency brake has gone out. We don't enter the structure, though. Something about it bothers me. The sandstone walls surrounding the circular interior, the two turrets on either side of the large bay window. Supposedly the hallways radiate out from the central staircase like spokes on a wheel. There are tales of the place being haunted, but everyone says they are happy ghosts. The Pittocks had six children and eighteen grandchildren. Henry came from Pennsylvania, penniless at age nineteen. Georgiana came from Keokuk, Iowa – in the opposite corner of the state from my hometown. I can't bring myself to look at empty rooms where a happy family once resided.

Instead we walk around the lawn. A group of artists has set up easels, situated them so they can overlook the city.

I watch their fingers grip small pieces of chalk, or charcoal or brushes. I look at Matt's hands and try to detect a twitch, a longing. Because I want him to long for something, even if it isn't for me.

    I place my hands on the split rail fence edging the property. The style of it seems out of place. I'd expect white picket, or tall posts with elegant wire strung between. This fence reminds me that Oregon hasn't forgotten its place in the West. While I've always seen this city as distinctive, a Shangri-La of sorts, it occurs to me now that while it may have risen above its roots, it has not forgotten them.

    Portland prides itself on being at the frontier of change in America: it is the greenest city in terms of politics and environmentalism and Cycling magazine ranked it "No.1 cycling city in America." The park I just jogged through is the largest urban wilderness in the country. And yet, when I took a carriage tour through downtown, our guide pointed out two adjoining parks that less than fifty years ago were segregated by gender. She also pointed out that while Portland boasts the largest urban park, it also has the smallest: it measures two feet across and holds a few tufts of flowers.

    I turn to smile at Matt and hoist myself up onto the top rail of the fence like I used to as a child in Colorado. My small hands holding out a round red apple for the neighbors' horses. While jogging earlier, I had passed by an apple tree growing so incongruously in the space between the sidewalk and the street. The fruit was yellow, ripe, ready to eat. I picked one and devoured it on the way back to Matt's and that is what I think of, now, as I hand Matt my camera to immortalize this moment: a woman alone in the frame, legs dangling off a fence. A smile caused by a stolen moment that I have kept all to myself.

In addition to the rocks, the Child collected postcards at every shop she visited. Urban or natural landscape: it did not matter. She kept them in a box underneath her corporeal bed, and looked at them when she missed the stars. Reminded herself why the New Place, and all other places that she shuffled her small feet across, were worth all that she had given up to be here.

Small Heat to Sustain Me

Five miles into the trip and the cab of the truck already smells of cat urine. Wedged behind the seats are plastic grocery bags of pitas, hummus, wheat crackers, tuna, and canned energy drinks, which we hope will sustain us for the next three days. From between the bucket seats, where I have stacked the cat carriers on top of each other, I hear the younger of my two cats yowling with displeasure because he has already given in to incontinence. This is not an ideal travel situation for any of us.

But what do I know of journeys? Mine is a life measured by what has not been done. In a small notepad I always keep with me are lists of records I have not bought, books I have not read, places I have yet to see. And just like everything else in my life, I have chosen to define even myself by what I am not. I am not the same young girl who once walked over the interstate bridge to hang out in downtown Omaha, to soak up the energy of an urban environment. After living for a year in Portland, all I want is to see some grasslands, an endless ocean, or an endless horizon. Confined by buildings and forests and underbrush and clouds, by sidewalks and umbrellas and Subaru Outbacks - I now miss what I once referred to as "the prison of open spaces."

Afraid to even attempt driving until I was nineteen, I am now, at 27, behind the wheel of a U-haul, pulling a trailer through the mountains of Montana. I had moved to Oregon to fill a perceived hole and discovered only more of them. When I first visited the city, it was the presence of things that drew me: friends, sushi bars, hiking trails – and only an hour's drive to the sea. But what was absent made me want to return: anxiety, restlessness, stagnation. Never having been satisfied with the places that chose me, I wanted to choose a place of my own this time, and the Pacific Northwest seemed to beckon.

The void is a compelling force, and humans will chase it to the ends of the earth. In Mark Danielewski's novel, <u>House of Leaves</u>, a literal void appears in a photojournalist's house. Like any good obsession, it lacks dimensions and fails to adhere to the known rules of time and space. "Sometimes," he writes, "it's even just a vapor trail speeding west, prophetic, over clouds aglow with dangerous light."

I am not speeding west, but east – a fact made apparent by the North Dakota state trooper who pulls me over in the vast stretch of badlands to write me a forty-dollar ticket. I'm barely speeding fast enough to make it worth the state's while. Next to me, my friend is roused from a nap she was taking, with her head resting against the window and a bright red boom box balanced on her lap: our solution to the lack of a cd player. She doesn't understand why I'm smiling, but it's my first speeding ticket ever, and I've earned it while driving a big truck, towing my car across the country in the middle of winter.

We ease back onto the road. It feels like I haven't seen any colors besides white, pink, and brown for many miles now, but in reality the badlands have a diverse palette of reds and rusts and browns. It's just difficult to appreciate the subtle, muted colors when I am used to so much green. Still, I've never been to this state, and it's a shame that I'm simply passing through, with only receipts and sheets of paper to remind me that I've been here at all.

Among the islands of Newfoundland, when it was time to move, when the land was no longer giving or forgiving, the islanders took their houses with them. Towropes were attached to the corners of the foundation, and large rafts were built to float them across the ocean. The scene I imagine is two lines of ten men in thick wool sweaters, rough rope over their shoulders, dragging a house up the rocky shore as if it were some new creature evolved from the sea. The beams crack and moan, shifting their weight, dispersing their energy down the long length of rope and throughout the men's bones. The sea roars, and then sighs. She wanted to pull them all down before their transient nature got the best of them, before they created too many voids, too many gaps in the chain to sustain them.

Behind us, I can see the orange trailer that holds the front end of my car shifting toward the centerline as we drive. In the back of the truck, hastily stacked boxes of books rearrange themselves as I take corners too tightly for such a long load. It doesn't help our cause that the U-haul is half-empty. If I hadn't purchased an expensive futon in Portland, I'd have been able to transport the four of us and all of our belongings in a couple of cars. Most of my books have been in storage boxes for years, maybe never to be read again. Like the people of Newfoundland, I am towing my whole life behind me, with a little help from friends.

We're traveling north to avoid the storm, the record-breaking supercell that is sweeping across five states. Nebraska and Wyoming are buried under two feet of snow, all the interstates are closed, and South Dakota, just miles away from us, is covered in a sheet of ice. Power lines are falling, candles are being lit, prayers are being sent out into the void. In their houses, families watch as whiteness descends, and they are dazzled as they remember how blinding it is, how it is almost as threatening as the dark.

On the road, nearing Minnesota now, my traveling companion and I pull over at a rest stop, where there are about ten semi trucks and us in the lot. She waits for me outside as I set up a hasty litter box and let the cats loose in the cab, hoping they'll get the hint. The older one does, the younger one claws at the window and yells, his fur bristling, shivering at the unknown. It's as if he wants out, but if I opened the door, I am sure he wouldn't move, stuck in the paradox of fearing something yet craving it at the same time.

Together, TaMara and I run through the pools of streetlight into the rest area, keys interlaced between our fingers. The bulbs in the stalls are flickering, which is nothing new, but makes us bear down on our bladders that much harder. Outside, of course, no one is waiting for us, no one even stirs, no cab lights flick on, no boots crunch on the icy gravel of the parking lot. Still, we jog back to the truck and lock ourselves in before pulling back onto the road.

I have always been drawn to stories of isolated places; to harsh landscapes that one must live with instead of just live in. Wyoming, Alaska, Newfoundland, Patagonia. The summer before I moved to Portland, I spent two weeks in Shell, Wyoming. A geologist's playground, the land lies in a basin between five mountain ranges, and due to glacial processes I can no longer recall, many layers of rock are exposed. It is an arid landscape, with hearty plants like alfalfa, saltbush, prickly pear, and wild onion springing up out of cracks in the clay. A five minute walk to the local café every morning got me covered in dust. The longest hangover of my life was in Wyoming, due to constant dehydration. It rained, even in torrents once, but by the next day the mud was caked and cracked. Annie Proulx says about Wyoming, "I have an intense interest in rough country and the people it makes, and that interest is satisfied here." Perhaps then, my own interest lies in what 'rough country' will make of me.

It's my turn to nap, but instead I tune in to NPR. The radio waves are coming to us from Fargo in the form of a cheeky narrator who seems to have had lessons from Garrison Keillor, and entertainment by "The Church Basement Ladies". We wait for the call-in section and are sorely disappointed when no one has an accent remotely close to the one in the movie. The folks I've met from southern Minnesota come closer than these guys.

We mull over stopping at a bar just to say we met someone from Fargo, but with valuables plus cats in the truck, it's really not an option. The crackly, amped buzz from the energy drinks is as impaired as we're going to get tonight. But the road is so dark and so straight that no matter who drives we keep drifting onto the rumble strips. We just want the spontaneity after so much stagnation.

The summer I was thirteen, my father, stepmother and I took a trip to Maine to visit her aging aunt. We were holed up for a week in a little town on the coast. It was summer, a mild sixty degrees, and there were other tourists in town. Every morning the fog would descend, but by noon it would lift and roll back out to sea. Couples rode bicycles down the wooded trail near our hotel, and just off shore, seals' heads would occasionally bob above the water. I was enchanted with the place, but I could see in the locals' faces that life was not always this easy, here, that their place on this rocky shore had been earned. Shuttling between states every summer, I had no idea where my place was, I still don't, but I knew I wanted to earn it, too.

The purpose of our trip to Maine was to visit Aunt Esther, but because it was in lieu of our usual summer vacation, we took a lobster boat out to sea. The sky was gray, and the water echoed its color. I stood at the rail, with my rain jacket zipped up tight, my long hair turning damp from the ocean mist and clinging to the sides of my face. The men showed us how they pulled the traps, and most were empty but a few were full. And while most of the tourists gathered around as the guide displayed a pregnant female, I was watching a gull circle low over the waves.

We'd only gone out a mile or two, if that, but you could barely see the shore. And then without warning, there was fog, thick and dense like I had never seen. Of course, it was nothing unusual in Camden, and the guide just smiled as he saw my hands tighten and turn white against the railing. There was a ten-foot radius of water around the boat, which seemed to shrink the world. And the resounding ding-ding of the buoy – a faint flash of red through the mists.

TaMara and I stay overnight in southern Minnesota, too weary to push on. It's drizzling when we wake up, but by the time we finish our third continental breakfast in a row, the drizzle is nearly a downpour. Thirty miles into Iowa, almost home, the rain lightens again and is replaced with fog. I am thrown back into that grey, rocky coastline, that first trip where I really connected with place, and I try to recall what it was that made the scene stick with me, and what it is I'm trying to make stick now. But memory is just as elusive as the weather, just as temporary and shrouded as the air on the other side of the window glass.

TaMara takes her socks off and puts her wide bare feet on the dash. She sighs, and rests her head on her fist, closes her eyes for lack of anything outside to look at. I don't mind if she falls asleep. There's no chance of being pulled over this time. We're not speeding, anymore, toward anything. We are simply sending the dim beams forth into the semi-dark, with just enough of a sense of what lies ahead to get us there.

When the water beckoned, the Child answered. It was like high diving from a very high place. She visualized the connection point and leaped: like an electron thrown out of orbit. Like salmon, swimming upstream. Like a stone, skipping across the glassy surface of a lake before settling into freefall toward the depths, the dark, the unknown.

Anesthetic

Out where the road turns to gravel is where you'll find it. A giant rock quarry on the left, filled in with a gray sort of sludge; and on the right, at least one square mile of barbed wire fencing, razor wire coiled above the chain link, obscuring the view of the brick guard towers that look like something out of a video game involving short swords and knights. In a reversal of fortune, however, it is my prince who is waiting to be rescued from this tower, and I, a chain smoking princess standing in the parking lot in the cold November air willing myself to go inside.

But I do it. And it isn't so bad. It's like the airport, only without a line – merely a bored guard with coifed blond hair staring at her fingernails and smacking gum as I walk through. I'm waiting for the director to yell 'cut,' but instead it's eerily quiet, so I keep walking the path they tell me, through gate after automated gate. I get buzzed into the visiting room by a short man in a white collared shirt and he easily sizes me up as fresh meat.

"Relationship to the offender?" he asks.

I say friend with confidence, but he just shakes his head.

"Friend with a grin." He pretends to study the half sheet of paper I have given him with Brian's DOC information on it and a circled number 'one,' meaning me, and tells me to follow his 'worker,' an inmate in gray prison pants and a white t-shirt, to a cushioned vinyl bench where I am assigned to wait for my 'friend' for agonizing minutes.

I have driven the long four hours down here on my psychiatrist's advice. He gave it to me nine years ago, and I've been 'sleeping on it' since then. Traveling back and forth across the country, trying to shake the shadows I was sure I could simply leave behind. But Brian's letters continued to find me even in the dead of winter in Oregon. Or tales of his failed phone calls to my mother's house. With or without my acknowledgement, my past existed and if I wanted a future, I was going to have to face it.

I aspire to work with gifted students someday, especially those at risk of straying from a successful path. But someone once asked me how I could heal others if I hadn't first healed myself? I had accomplished things, yes. And my body was fine. Hell, I was training to run a marathon. But spiritually and emotionally I was still full of holes, and in order to truly do the good work I wanted to do in the world, I was going to have to fill them in, or be stuck in a sort of limbo state forever.

I sit alone on the vinyl bench for what seems like hours but is actually only about thirty minutes. Brian doesn't know that I'm coming on this day. I've chosen to surprise him. So he won't be prepared and waiting in his cell for the guards to come get him. When he does arrive, his face looks first confused, then shocked, then elated. I go up to the white taped off area to greet him and the comfort of his arms tells me the only story I really needed to know. He doesn't want to let go. Or rather, he hasn't let go, in all these years of a love I thought was lost to another possible universe, forever.

We walk in silence back to our assigned seat and for a while he just stares at me while I stare out the window.

"What?" I ask and he grins that infamous grin.

"Nothing. I'm just looking at you." He pauses. "Wow."

His voice takes on a sort of breathless quality, like a six year old who has just come downstairs on Christmas morning to find a bright shiny bicycle, complete with a bell just waiting to be rung.

I have a hard time looking at him for fear of being overcome by an affection that had lain long dormant. Instead I sneak glances out of the corner of my eye. Become defensive. We make sarcastic jokes at each other and though I was sure I would cry, we laugh and laugh for the whole two hours.

Brian has done well for himself, in as much as was possible. He hit a low point, much like I did, where he had to choose to either take control of the rest of his life or succumb to despair entirely. He chose, as did I, to rise. Now he is a peer mentor for younger guys in the substance abuse program, he has an office job at the metal shop, and he is a spiritual leader for the Wiccan community inside. He has read voraciously, more even than I, and he writes short stories in his long hours of spare time. He has learned to play guitar and plays in two bands, is on a softball team in the summer, and lifts weights. And he is eternally optimistic about his life after these final four years are over with. His eyes are bright, his hands are warm, and his face radiates a cautious hope.

"Prison changes a man," everyone tells me, but it isn't true this time. He has grown, yes, but in ways that are good and solid. Like me, he has lived these past years clutching a dream close to his heart and refusing to let them take it from him. And now, it seemed, the dream might just come true.

I finished that pack of cigarettes on the drive back to Iowa - the first I had relished in years. And then I moved to Kansas City the next summer and inhabited the ghost of Brian's life. I cleaned out his closets, filling garbage bags full of clothes that his 15 year old self used to wear and I imagined he would not want at thirty-five. I rifled through and organized old photos, some of which I was in. I pored over the court documents and law books and online forums trying desperately to find a way to reduce his time.

Finally, I realized that the dream was just that. I was happy for my Loki, and the peace he had found in his long hours of solitude behind bars. I was glad he had a wonderful family who was anxiously waiting for him to come home. But my shoes in his old closet and my pictures on the wall – they didn't seem to fit. The girl in the mirror wasn't the girl in the old photos anymore. And the young man – well, he was gone, too.

There is a void in each of us that is all our own. No other can be a salve or salvation. I said good-bye over the phone, and cried the whole three-hour drive back to my once again home in Iowa. I left his possessions behind, and a few of mine, just in case he still needed a bit of that dream to hold to the light when the shadows were long and the days were short. I had no idea what I still needed to find, but I was finally beginning to understand what I hadn't. I pointed the car down another gravel road, and gently infused the engine with gas.

Before Loki was a god, he was a spider on a string, a coyote howling at the moon. Before Sigyn was a Halfling, she was a swan, gliding in circles under the sun. Before the Child was a child, she was a bird (and also a griffin, a heroine, a fawn). Be-fore there was water there was air. We walk before we can crawl.

Clawed Feet

At first it was just a speck in the distance, and then it began to take shape. A grayish form hunched over a victim not its own; right on the dividing line between the westbound lanes of the Kansas-10. It was the first to arrive, before even the ants, and it had claimed this carcass, traffic be damned. A lone scavenger in mid-morning in the middle of the road. We saw each other, disregarded each other. And that turned out to be a mistake.

I had gotten up that morning and put on the coffee as usual. Read the NY Times online, threw in a load of laundry, showered, and prepared to visit a friend I hadn't seen in over a year. Alexa and I met when we both lived and worked in Portland, Oregon, and now our paths had converged near the wheatfields of Kansas and the great Missouri River. It was fortuitous that fate brought us within driving distance, and we were excited to see each other again.

It was a blue-sky day. The kind of blue you only find in places that once were prairie: bright like robin's eggs, fading to white near the horizon. A good day for traveling. A day where bad omens are completely unexpected. But is the vulture really a bad omen? I saw it from about a mile away, its hunched form, wings bent like shoulders over its victim, neck long and crooked, eyes intent on what would be, if it weren't confined to scavenging, its prey.

There are those who theorize that humans were scavengers once. That in our first faltering steps upright we lacked the agility or sensory reflexes to hunt. What we did have, these anthropologists say, is intelligence, and it was this trait that kept us alive where others had failed. Perhaps the same holds true for the vulture. According to the Red Creek Wildlife Center in Pennsylvania, "Of all the wild animals we handle, vultures possess a noticeable intelligence... only seen rivaled by parrots." Parrots who seem to hold a key to another human trait that ensured our survival: language.

Why, then, didn't this particular bird ensure his own survival? He looked up, saw the metal beasts coming towards him, and returned to the rotting feast. Only when I was a few short feet away did he lift his heavy body in an attempt at flight, meeting my windshield with a crack. I couldn't swerve or brake, for other vehicles were both next to me and behind me, so I kept going, stunned, looking for his body to fall aside in the rear view, but it did not. He flew away, probably with ribs broken, and surely to die.

In Native American mythology, animal totems are a large part of the belief system. Totem animals make themselves known to the individual, and become that individual's spirit guide. The individual is chosen by the significant being, not the other way around. Because vultures are scavengers, they are seen as residing between the worlds of the living and the dead. They perpetuate the cycle of life, by breaking down the spoils of others' kills. To have one enter your life as a spirit guide, then, is actually considered a good omen. The vulture provides balance between positive and negative forces. He navigates the currents effortlessly using the most minimal effort possible, and in turn, will help the chosen individual navigate the emotional currents of his or her life.

So there I was on a blue-sky day, somewhere between starting a new future and reminiscing about the past with an old friend. We were, both of us, uncertain where the currents of life were about to take us. But as my winged friend reminded me, many great beasts have walked these same paths before us, and many will follow in our wake. Tomorrow morning I will put on another pot of coffee, read the NY Times online, fold and put away the laundry. I will cycle back through old patterns, make the same mistakes or make new ones, rekindle old friendships and forge new relationships. And in some blue or not so blue sky above me will be a vulture, gaunt and homely, effortlessly riding the currents, circling for an ending life to shepherd into death, showing me the way.

In the rainbow, colors bleed together. From the small box, the Child watches them dance on the wall, thinks of darkness, thinks of light. She does not think of color. She cannot contain it in conception. She does not think of texture, either, having lived so long in transitional places, she has forgotten what it feels like to just be. When she is restless, she reaches out her tiny hand – trusting whatever reaches back to be true.

The Endless Blue of the Sky

I just spent part of a windy winter morning searching for stones along the shore of Lake Superior. In part because I have always liked collecting rocks, especially beach rocks – but also because the local culture has a tradition of collecting agates. The official state gemstone, agates here have a different tone than agates found elsewhere, I am told. Here – they are red, orange, yellow, brown-gold – instead of the usual blue to whitish grey (as my guide to gemstones saved from a college course informs me). In fact, the banding and color of the Lake Superior agates makes them perfect choices for use in Cameo medallions – which I also loved to collect as a child.

    I was wary of walking along the rocky beach, but the stones piled by the tides were solid and did not shift under my feet as I had imagined they would. The larger rocks were covered in ice. The wind was strong enough to make whitecaps on the waves. But kneeling down to gather the small stones protected me from the coldest part of it.

    I remember one of my favorite books as a child was the story of a young girl and her grandmother digging mussels out of the sand. In the illustrations, the girl had a metal pail and a small plastic shovel. The wind blew her hair out behind her as her grandmother walked behind. The mussels were large and grey and unappetizing – and yet I wanted to inhabit that story. I read it over and over again, hearing in my mind the sound of waves on rocks, feeling my toes dig into the sand. Showing off my bucket of treasure to a waiting matriarch.

    Here, I have no bucket, no grandmother, nor is this the sea. And the rocks are of no use, really, except as decorations in a glass jar. But somehow, to me, the work seems the same – and perhaps it is the work that is important. For just as in the story, it requires searching for something that would stay hidden otherwise. It requires a humbling, a kneeling down, and a confrontation with certain elements.

Stone as metaphor, of course carries with it a weight. Virginia Woolf put stones in her pockets and walked into water. Stones are seen as burdens, or loads – so collecting them seems the opposite of a fruitful endeavor. And yet – stones can also be a foundation, or represent being found. The Irish still build their fences and sometimes their houses of stones. Stone cairns mark the way for lost hikers in the desert and mountains.

And then there is that other childhood story: "Stone Soup." Various versions of the folk tale exist, I am sure, but in the one I remember best a young man arrives at an old woman's door, hungry and tired. The woman, too, is poor, and denies food to her guest – until he eventually tricks her with a tale of stone soup. All he needs is a pot and some water, and he will make soup from a stone. As he heats his simple dish, and begins to feast on it, he laments how it would be better with a little garnish – this or that, until eventually the woman has contributed her stock of vegetables to the brew and soon they both feast on a hearty meal.

It's a perfect story for this time of year – when expectations sometimes force our miserly natures out into the open. And even more perfect for me, because, like the young boy in the story, I am a stranger on these shores. And I am already out taking tokens of her bounty in the form of these small stones. "Treasure hunting," a tourism brochure called it.

I don't even have a jar for them yet. They are sitting in a small pile on the kitchen table, and every time I look at them I have half a mind to go put them back. Then again, I came here to become part of this place – and if that means spending time kneeling down on beds of stones, searching for small ones that stand out, then I will gladly put in the work. Stockpiling the local treasure like cords of wood, or like the little gray and red squirrels stockpile the nuts we leave out for them on the deck.

I only meant to go for a walk this morning. I did not intend on filling my pockets with these stones. But the anthropologist in me was intrigued by the stories of this strange treasure-hunting ritual and that is how I wound up on my knees. I suppose I am hoping that someday a local will see my filled-up jar and nod and smile and accept that I have earned my place in this northern culture by spending a sufficient amount of time at fruitless tasks. Or that I can conjure up the base to a hearty soup with them – when the whitecaps turn to ice and the cold reaches the marrow of my bones. Or perhaps this one winter morning will never amount to anything but an anomaly. A young woman picking her way through rocks on a strange new shore, her hair blown back by the wind, her pockets deep and empty and ready to take on this new weight, one small stone at a time.

EPIGRAPH: SCARS

I tried to make the engagement work, but instead found myself dredged through layers of the past until they started to knit together like sutures that would finally allow me to heal. I literally went through all of Brian's things and removed the unnecessary reminders that would be, we agreed, obstacles to his adjusting to life as a 37 year old man who had been in prison since before he was even old enough to drink. But it may have been, ultimately, and despite best intentions, more for my benefit than his. I was living my life as a fatalist, waiting for the sky to fall, the inevitable slice of Occam's Razor.

The letters still come. The texts from pilfered cell phones. The images in my sleep of the two lonely steel-toed boots that I left in his closet, the ones I wore to prom under my dress, the ones that hung over the edge of that dock so long ago. I hope that his mother has had the good sense to throw them out by now.

Now, I have come to learn that life is, instead, defined by our choices, not by chance occurrences. I am still a mystic, still read Tarot and light sage and dance to drums on full moons on the beach. I subscribe to my horoscope more than a little lightly. But I also understand that in large part, my suffering had been caused by the choices I made to indulge it – by a view of the world formed when my family unknit itself when I was seven and no one ever sat me down to explain that it wasn't luck or fate or a little girl at the root of it.

My sister slammed my finger in a closet door when I was four. The nail turned black, fell off at the root. It grew back, and no scar remains. I fell on the playground at six or seven and hobbled on a skinned knee for weeks. The knee is still pale pink in the crease, still echoes of the pain it once felt. My forearms are free of the hope I tried to gouge out of them, but my thumb lacks nerve endings that never grew back. My stomach is strong, my heart is weak, my feet beat the path ever forward.

There are holes in this narrative that I can't suture together. I was born in Iowa, born on the wind, raised in the mountains, caravanned across the country, and have finally landed by a great lake, which I now call home. Alone. There are ghosts in my bedroom, but rarely any flesh. There is a woman in my skin who is still a little girl. There is a song in my heart that still sings for the one who was meant to hear it: that lucky fool.

There is a crack in everything. That's how the light gets in.
- Leonard Cohen

Acknowledgements:

This book began as the idle dream of a little girl looking down upon the world from a waiting star. She found me and whispered it into my ear and has now disappeared back into a world more magical than this one. I have merely filled in the unremembered bits of her story with remembered bits of my own.

The following people had a hand in the remembering and rendering: Sarah Pett – my 'person' and spiritual sister; Melanny Henson – medium, editor, goddess, and late night wine companion; My mother – the first to believe in me; My father – for always encouraging me to keep reading; Steve Pett, Debra Marquart, and Mary Swander – for teaching me "the craft" and reading multiple drafts; Joyce Brandt Clark – for introducing me to the planet Beyond; Eldon Johnston, Jr. – for advising me to "tell it like it is"; Brian 'Loki' Campbell – for his unwavering faith and letters; Jesse Woodward – for showing me how to dream again; Sharon Drake Spinharney for not letting me kill the bunny, AND, of course, the *desaparecidos* without whom I would never have understood the beautiful depths of loss…

Jennifer Lee Clark
    b. May 2, 1978   d. May 2, 1978
Madison Renae Clark
    b. December 27, 2002   d. January 24, 2003
Nicole Reanin Elgan-Moore
    b. January 28, 1980   d. July 25, 2005

And countless others…above and below…I hope you know who you are. XO

Made in the USA
Lexington, KY
24 March 2017